CHELSEA BONNER

BODY IMAGE Warrior

Published in 2019 by Murdoch Books, an imprint of Allen & Unwin

Murdoch Books Australia
83 Alexander Street, Crows Nest NSW 2065
Phone: +61 (0)2 8425 0100
murdochbooks.com.au
info@murdochbooks.com.au

Murdoch Books UK
Ormond House, 26–27 Boswell Street, London WC1N 3JZ
Phone: +44 (0) 20 8785 5995
murdochbooks.co.uk
info@murdochbooks.co.uk

A catalogue record for this book is available from the National Library of Australia

A catalogue record for this book is available from the British Library
ISBN 978 1 76052 381 7 Australia

Cover photography by Michelle Holden

Printed and bound in Australia by Griffin Press

10 9 8 7 6 5 4 3 2

The paper in this book is FSC® certified. FSC® promotes environmentally responsible, socially beneficial and economically viable management of the world's forests.

CHELSEA BONNER

BODY IMAGE *Warrior*

MURDOCH BOOKS
SYDNEY · LONDON

For Maria, who has asked me every week for eight years,
'when are you going to write a book?'

PROLOGUE

It's the 2011 Miami launch of the *Sports Illustrated* Swimsuit Issue cover and I find myself at a final-night party on a luxury superyacht surrounded by stars, models and crew. It's a dizzying collection of the world's most beautiful people, including Gigi Hadid, Chrissy Teigen, Ashley Graham, Hannah Ferguson, Rose Bertram, Chanel Iman, Bojana Krsmanovic and my own *BELLA* model, Robyn Lawley.

There is dancing on the oversized roof deck, the Champagne is flowing freely and everyone is in high spirits at the end of a demanding week.

I've been to a few of these Swimsuit Issue wrap parties before and they are always fun. Everyone is letting off steam after a stressful, fast-paced week packed with nonstop make-up and wardrobe changes on the most stunning women on the planet. The shoot tends to bring out all the usual personality clashes, diva demands and unpredictable challenges that come from photographing supermodels in the outdoors, so it's no wonder that the excitement and release at the wrap party is palpable. This night, however, I feel more than the usual relief and satisfaction at being involved in another edition of this iconic magazine: this year I feel exhilarated and full of hope and pride. This year is special, because it's the first time in the history of the magazine that they have featured a plus-size model on the cover.

There is Ashley Graham, the unapologetically real and undeniably gorgeous American supermodel, giving one of the bestselling magazines in the USA all the sultriness, sexiness and spectacular beauty it could handle. At home in Australia, Robyn Lawley had just shot for *Vogue* Australia — the first plus-size model in its 52-year history. The combination of these two extraordinary feats made the vindication I had been working towards for my entire career complete. Ashley and Robyn were out there representing everything I knew to be true about beauty and diversity, and they were proving it in a way that couldn't be ignored.

All my life I have fought against the idea that there is one set of requirements for feminine beauty. As a teenage girl whose body developed curves when fashion dictated that thin was in; as a young working woman who was constantly judged by society to be less worthy or capable because of her weight; as a plus-size model being forced to wear ill-fitting, baggy clothes which sent the less-than-subtle message that a larger body should be hidden; and as a successful businesswoman working in the fashion and beauty industry, being forced to watch young women ruin their health and their lives while they desperately tried to measure up to unattainable expectations set by unrealistic ideals.

I have always believed that all women deserve to feel good about themselves, no matter what size they are. Women don't deserve to be judged as less worthy or less deserving of respect and love because of their size. Beauty isn't one-size-fits-all and it was time that the fashion and beauty industries accepted that truth. Watching Ashley and my gorgeous curve model Robyn shine alongside all the other supermodels on the yacht that night felt like a paradigm shift. Perhaps we really can find a new way to see beauty. Perhaps we can all be body image warriors and the world will finally see women's beauty for what it is — real.

In the spotlight. My parents at a party for all the beautiful people, Sydney 1972, two years before I was born.

CHAPTER 1

I was an unusually ugly baby, according to my Nana, who wasn't one to mince words. You would have thought my squished, lopsided face and crooked neck would make me one for Nana's affection, but perhaps the contrast between my average appearance and the polished glamour of my model mother and movie-star father was too great for her to reconcile. She had been known to tell me directly that she couldn't believe two such beautiful people could produce such an ugly child. To her surprise though, I grew out of that 'ugly duckling' stage and developed the blue eyes, blonde ringlets and dimples she had expected from birth: a right little Shirley Temple.

I was born in the leafy Melbourne suburb of Kew, just past midnight on 18th March, 1974. A Pisces baby, and a very happy one by all accounts, I was also completely innocent of any knowledge of the family I had been born into.

In Australia in the 1970s and 80s there were few couples who could outshine my genetically gifted parents. My mother, Nola Clark, was a model and my father, Tony Bonner, was one of Australia's biggest television and film actors.

Mum was 'discovered' at the age of 16, working in a Myer department store. As part of her job for the junior Miss Shop section of the store, she was often asked to try on samples of the clothes for fashion buyers. It was during one of these in-house presentations that Steve Bennett, a sales manager for fashion label Trent Nathan, spotted her and she was scouted on the spot as a model. From this moment my mother's world changed. She went from being a regular 16-year-old suburban teenager with an interest in fashion, to beauty pageants and catwalk shows around the world, winning the 'Quest of Quests' in Sydney and going on to be first runner-up in Miss International in Japan in 1972. Mum appeared on the covers of so many magazines that I've lost count. She became the darling of photographers and clients because of her hardworking ethic and down-to-earth nature. She landed huge national advertising jobs like the 'Busy Girl' shampoo and hairspray campaign, which still gets her recognised in the street today. Mum's modelling career saw her move from Melbourne to Sydney and then to London. Even after she and Dad were married and moved back to Australia to start a family, she continued to feature on the covers of the best-selling women's magazines. She has been a highly sought-after model throughout my entire life.

In the late 60s and 70s Dad starred in the iconic Australian TV series *Skippy the Bush Kangaroo*, *Cop Shop* and *Skyways*. In the 1980s he played roles in internationally lauded films like

The Man from Snowy River and *The Lighthorsemen,* as well as the hugely popular miniseries *Anzacs* and regular TV series *Carson's Law*. All in all, Dad has appeared in more than 30 films, 25 television series and many short film and voice over roles. During my childhood my father was one of Australia's most well-known and well-respected film and television actors.

Around the time Mum moved to Sydney to pursue her modelling career she found herself knocking on the door of a friend's house for a party. It was opened by Dad and the romance began. It was 1971.

...

As a child I looked forward to every opportunity to tag along on a job with my parents. I loved the idea that you could go somewhere for a few hours or a few months and be someone else for a time. It was like the minute I walked through the door, I could feel the energy shift and suddenly, I was in the middle of somebody's dream or wild imagining. I especially loved watching the transformation of the models. Everything from hair and make-up to the sets and lights which made them appear like otherworldly creatures. I would watch, transfixed by their innate understanding of where to place their hands or feet. Every gesture was perfect, like a silent dance that brought a character and a scene to life.

While Mum's work was an exciting whirlwind of make-up, set lighting and hairspray, Dad's was on a different level and another world entirely. The sets were enormous, and there was a cast of hundreds involved in some of the more famous productions. I remember being an eight-year-old on set with

Dad during the filming of *The Man from Snowy River* in Victoria's high country. I was in heaven among the horses and dust and flies. I loved feeling like I was a part of the action. I would follow the cast and crew to the Merrijig pub for roast dinner when shooting was done for the day. The crew would order their beers and I'd be given a raspberry and lemonade, otherwise known as a 'Shirley Temple'. Sometimes I would be given a job to do, like when I was asked to brush star Tom Burlinson's horse between takes. On the set of *The Lighthorsemen* I was fed bacon and eggs for breakfast by Paul Hogan and, in a tragic twist, was one of the few people to see the star-on-the-rise Jon Blake before he was horrifically injured in a car crash at the end of filming.

Film sets were an exhilarating and exciting insight into a make-believe world and if I could have lived on set I would have. Perhaps if I could stay in these charmed worlds then my childhood would have been happy. Unfortunately, the cameras always stopped rolling, the cast and crew returned home, and real life crashed in over the top of the fantasy. The truth of my life during these times was far from the perfect image the media portrayed of my parents. In reality, the celebrity our parents brought to our lives was a heavy burden for us all to bear.

...

I have two younger sisters: Skye, who is just 18 months younger than me, and Hanna, who is five years younger. I was very protective of my little sisters when we were small. I would call Skye 'my baby' and when Hannah got older and more interactive I would dress her up in costumes — anything cute that would show off her beautiful blonde curls. We all had different ways of coping with life at home when we were children. For me, I became a dreamer who loved magical things and believed with all my heart that fairies lived in the garden outside my bedroom window. I loved to escape to this imaginary world, where the fairies would tell me their secrets and would get me into all sorts of trouble by suggesting naughty things for us to do. I had vivid dreams, in which I would leave my sleeping body and fly down the street to visit friends as they slept, saying hello to all the animals in my neighbours' yards. Each night I would kiss all my teddy bears and dolls before I went to sleep, making sure to never leave anyone out. They all had to have an equal amount of love, because I knew they would watch over me and keep me safe during the night.

Starting primary school came with its own set of difficulties. I wasn't a bad student, but I didn't enjoy school. I would often hide away in a corner of the library with a book, only to be discovered by the librarian well after the bell had gone to return to class. Drop-off and pick-up times were the worst because that was when the other parents would come to gawk at Mum or, even more so, at Dad.

This was the side of fame that Dad hated. Being stopped every two steps for an autograph or surrounded by people who just wanted to stare at him. It was uncomfortable for all of us and always stressful for him, having to be 'on' for a crowd. We naturally picked up on his stress, and always felt anxious about his reaction to it. People lose their minds around famous people: normal mums and dads would become overly friendly and gushy to get his attention. I found it so awkward watching adults behave like that and I felt like the other kids were looking at me sideways, as though I expected the same from them.

School became a minefield of trying not to stand out. Other kids would often accuse me of showing off or thinking I was special. Of course, I was just a kid and, while I knew my parents' jobs weren't like the other parents' jobs, I didn't fully comprehend just *how different*; but the other children could sense the distinction and I was teased and bullied no end. When one of my classmate's mothers was featured in the paper because of her business the little girl brought the article into school for show and tell. I obviously didn't express enough excitement, which made her furious. The teasing lasted for a week or more; none of the other girls would play with me. It just hadn't occurred to me that being in the paper wasn't part of everyday life.

I found that spending time with boys helped me avoid problems with groups of girls. Boys were always so much more clueless about social cues. I loved sport and so I'd play basketball, softball and running races with the boys — they were less confusing to me. But the refuge I found in the company of boys or in sport was nothing compared to the happiness I experienced when I was with horses.

My love of horses started when I was very young. My aunt had horses, and as a toddler I would disappear and be found sitting in a paddock with them, sometimes under them. Because Dad was often filming with horses, it became my passionate and desperate wish to have my own. I seized every opportunity to be around them. I would sneak off to the paddocks at my grandparents' house up the road and spend hours playing with

My first appearance in Woman's Day, *as a newborn in 1974.*

them and begging rides from friends. One afternoon, when Dad was finishing filming *The Man from Snowy River*, a horse float turned up with a present for me. I was so excited: I was going to have my first pony! They unloaded the trailer and there he was: a small grey donkey called Giddy Up that Mum had leased for me as a gift for my eighth birthday. I didn't mind that it wasn't a pony. I had something to ride and that was all that mattered. I would proudly ride around the neighbourhood on that old donkey, bareback, because no-one had thought of buying me a saddle. Now, it makes me laugh to think what a sight the two of us must have been. Everyone in our neighbourhood rode these amazing show horses and competed at the Royal shows and here I was trotting along on Giddy Up, proud as punch. Unfortunately for Giddy Up, he didn't last long. He ate my Nana's trees and flowers, so he was shipped off home to his farm and Mum bought me my first real pony, Toffee. I had saved up $50 and Mum matched me dollar for dollar, but it turned out that Toffee wasn't much better behaved than Giddy Up. Having taught many children to ride during her life, she was now a cagey old thing and knew all the tricks in the book to dismount me. She'd swerve into fences to scrape my leg or bolt for low branches to swipe me off. We had to tie up her head with a hay band when we rode her, because otherwise she'd stop mid-canter to eat grass and whoever was riding would fly off over her head. I loved that pony to tears, though, and she made me an excellent rider. No horse alive could unseat me after riding Toffee.

I kept Toffee at my grandparents' place and, as a result, I spent as much time as possible there; there was nowhere else in the world I wanted to be. Back then, kids were let out of the house in the morning and all we had to do was be home by dark. It was very different to the life of a child today. I rode for hours by myself, through the orchards of Templestowe and Doncaster and all the way out to Donvale or Warrandyte. We rarely had to cross a road in those days. Sometimes I'd meet up with friends, but I was just as happy on my own. I loved the freedom. I had all sorts of accidents and bumps and scratches from slips and falls. Looking back now, I think it built up a self-reliance and confidence in me that I might not have developed otherwise. When life bucks you off, you just shake it off and get back on the ride: that's what I learnt from those experiences.

I was always drawn to animals, much more than people. I found humans confusing: there were so many expectations and rules of interaction. I was always super sensitive to the mood of the room I was in. It was as if I could feel who was sad, who was aggressive, who was silly, who was safe. If I was smiling, someone might say, 'What are you smiling about?' or, if I wasn't smiling: 'What's wrong with you? Cheer up.' If my sisters and I were having fun together we were too noisy and told that 'children should be seen and not heard' or 'go and play' or 'don't touch that!' Being such an empathetic and hyper-sensitive child made life confusing for me.

Animals, on the other hand, are only interested in your good heart. That's all that matters to them. In many ways, horses replaced the fairies of my early childhood. I felt free and safe whenever I was with them; enough that I could, momentarily, escape from the troubles at home.

CHAPTER 2

My parents were celebrities, but being a celebrity in Australia in the 1980s was not like being a celebrity today. People think that celebrity means money, and to this day many people believe we were millionaires when I was growing up. The truth, however, was that Australian celebrities don't earn anything like the money that actors and models in the United States do. Especially back then. There were no residuals in place for actors when my Dad was working and there were few roles on offer compared to the number of actors looking for work. It was always a matter of having to fight for the same three or four roles. So, on paper — or, should I say, 'in the paper'? — we looked solvent, but the jobs, though they paid better than most jobs, were very spaced out. It may have looked like $50,000 was a fortune for eight weeks' work, but it had to last us until the next big job, which could be two months away or even two years. We never knew. Mum's constant modelling work was what kept us afloat during those times.

Growing up, we lived in a very normal, middle-class neighbourhood. It was semi-rural — full of trees and dogs and kids. We never took an overseas holiday or anything that flash. We would spend most holidays somewhere in Victoria: staying with friends in the caravan park at Rosebud; on our friend's houseboat on Lake Eildon; or at my Aunty Karen's house in the country. We couldn't plan very far ahead because of our parents' work. We couldn't spend too much money at any one time because we never knew when more would be earned. I never minded our financial circumstances; as a child it never occurred to me to mind. As long as I was near, or on, a horse, or I was swimming or climbing trees or playing sport, I was happy. I remember one of my favourite holidays was when Mum hired a campervan and we drove around Victoria with the dogs.

Every Christmas we would get the same combination of gifts: a toy we really wanted, like my Barbie horse 'Dallas'; a new 'good' outfit or dress; and a stocking of sweets. Every Easter the bunny would leave us a large chocolate egg surrounded by little flavoured chocolates. Mum and Nana were good at sewing so they made our bedspreads, curtains, some of our clothes and Mum's evening wear, most notably her Logies outfits, which she designed herself every year. We saved money where we could so that Dad could go to Los Angeles every pilot season to audition. He was always hoping to land the next big role, the game-changing role of a lifetime that drives every actor.

Our home was comfortable and warm, and both my parents had excellent style. We had an above-ground pool in the backyard, a trampoline and trees to climb. My uncle built us a playroom extension, which we piled with beanbags and dress-up clothes. I remember it being just like the other houses in our neighbourhood. We were middle-class and normal from the outside. I still remember the smell of the garden in summer after it had been watered: the smell of the cold water hitting hot tanbark after a day in the sun. I remember the winters, sitting with our backs to the open fire in our nighties, drying our hair before bed. I loved the sound of the flames crackling and the smell of our clean hair as it dried.

These memories were real and tell of happy times when I was growing up, but there was more to our lives than this collection of reminiscences. Behind magazine covers and the Logies nights and the photos in the paper, our family kept a dark secret. As soon as we were behind closed doors, all the gloss disappeared and we were cornered in the dark trenches of my father's alcoholism.

My nights were filled with dread for most of my childhood. We never knew which side of my dad would walk through the door at the end of the day; it was a coin toss between the silly drunk who posed no threat, or the terrifying man we hardly recognised as our father. It was mostly the latter. Dad might have been battling his own demons, but at the very same time he became ours. I longed for someone to rescue us, but I was also terrified of telling anyone what was really going on. We all knew that it was our shameful secret.

In the evenings, when Dad had been at the pub, we would wait for the sound of his car crunching the gravel in the driveway. This was my cue to run into the hallway and look to

Mum. Her silent instruction was for me to hide. With this look, I'd run to my little sisters' room and lock the door behind me. If the sounds of fighting woke them up, I'd tell them stories and dress up as their favourite cartoon characters and jump around singing and laughing to mask the awful noise of slamming doors, thuds on walls and crying and yelling. I always had one ear out for the nuances of the yelling. Steady yelling was good: if Mum was angry, that was a good sign. The nights she was too scared to be angry and could be heard pleading, 'Please don't — the kids', quietly, over and over: those were the worst. Sometimes I'd creep up the hallway to see what was happening and there were times I'd launch myself at him to pull him off. Other times I'd be too late; then all that was left to do was pick Mum up off the floor like a little broken doll. Sometimes I was too scared to look at all and I'd wear the shame of that inaction like a heavy coat.

Every now and then the publican, or someone else who had seen Dad at the pub, would call our home in the evening to let us know when he was heading back: 'He'll be home soon, love.' This would give Mum and me time to get ourselves and the house ready. That included hiding Dad's collection of working rifles that were mounted in our living room. Often after a few drinks he'd pull them down and shoot beer cans and tree trunks in our backyard, but they were too risky a weapon to have lying around when he was on a drunken rampage.

It sounds like a crazy situation when I write about it now, but then it was just our normal. The children's bedroom doors locked, guns hidden while we waited. Mum in her room and

Miss International of 1971, Nola Clark, has been modelling for eight years.

About two and a half years ago she married actor Tony Bonner and now she has a daughter, Chelsea, 16 months, above, and is expecting her second child.

Nola, 23, says her work is a bit limited at the moment but she still does some photographic modelling — and of course models maternity wear.

She says her mother, who lives nearby, has helped her care for Chelsea and looked after her when Nola has been out on assignments.

Nola does mostly photographic modelling for advertisements.

'Miss International of 1971' aka Mum, with me.

me in mine, praying that it would be the sleepy drunk and not the ugly one, but never knowing which we would get until he walked in the door.

Dad could be dangerously unpredictable during the daytime as well as the evening; we were never sure what would set him off. It could be anything from a dinner he didn't like, to too much talking, one of us lazing in our room or hanging around too much and being in the way. We had to try to guess his mood and hope we gave the right reaction. Every time Dad went out drinking, I would pray he never made it home, and then I would feel sick with guilt about that thought. How can you love someone so much, and hate them so terribly at the same time? I don't know, but I did.

There were times at night when we didn't hear anything for hours and we would fall asleep thinking he was gone for a few days. But in the middle of the night I would wake up with a heavy shadow on the end of my bed. There was Dad, sitting still but speaking softly. I'd start and sit bolt upright, petrified. He would be wreathed in cigarette smoke and the smell of Scotch would fill the air. Then he'd begin to cry and tell me his worries, but it never made any sense to me. The stench of the booze and the fear I was feeling only added up to confusion in my young mind. I'd look around my room, with my little pink-and-white bed and matching curtains and feel absurdly angry at all my teddies and dolls because they had failed to protect me while I slept.

...

By the time I started the first year of high school, I was emotionally shattered. During the day I was going to school to be bullied and harassed by the older girls — the girls who thought I needed to be taken down a peg or two because of my parents' celebrity — and at home I was tiptoeing through landmines, never sure which comment would set one off.

That year I came down with glandular fever and had something of a breakdown. I'd never slept well at night before, but after this illness I was terrified to go to sleep. I didn't want to leave the house or even my room. Mum took me to doctor to try to get me to talk, but I couldn't articulate my feelings. They wanted to know what was going on, but how could I explain what I didn't know myself? All I knew was that my brain was telling me to *stay still, stay quiet, don't move, be small, don't make a noise and then no-one can pick on you.* Most importantly, don't tell 'the secret' of my father's alcoholism and abuse. I was just broken. Done in. I was 12 years old.

...

I seemed to aggravate the older girls at high school, just by being in the same room as them. As a result, I'd creep around the hallways, trying to hide in corners. Whispers of 'she thinks she's so good' and much worse always trailed behind me. I was covered in bruises from being thrown against the lockers every lunchtime. I was scared to go to school at all.

The only reason I went to school was to get away from home and to play sport. I was good at most sports, and they brought me the sense of achievement and belonging that I so badly craved. My teachers either loved me or hated me. I was a fickle

Chronic, toxic stress of the sort experienced by maltreated children, and particularly in the absence of consistent, supportive and interactive relationships with adult caregivers, has been found to have an especially deleterious effect on young children's growing brains.

'Effects of child abuse and neglect for children and adolescents', published online at aifs.gov.au, 2014 student: if I was interested in something I would give it everything I had, if not I would get bored and easily restless.

Many of the teachers and students at school had no idea which grade I was in. It was a big school, and seniors could be in free dress, so I often went to school in my uniform and then changed into street clothes once I got there. Very often I didn't even go to class, just hung around all day hiding in the shadows and trying to remain invisible until I had to go home again. I was rarely missed. Getting in trouble was nothing to me; I was already living in a war zone at home, so I certainly wasn't afraid that anything more could be done to me at school.

Outside sport it was horses, dogs and my best friend, Tarnia, that were my saviours. The animals gave me as much love as they received, and animals always provided an escape from it all. When I was with them I was happy and the noises in my head quietened.

Tarnia and I were horse-mad tomboys who also loved books and horror movies. If we weren't out with the horses we would be in her bedroom reading book after book; stopping to eat or lean out of her window to sneak a cigarette, careful to blow the smoke outside so her parents couldn't smell it in the room. Sometimes we'd scare ourselves stupid watching horror films alone in her big house. I never told her what was going on at home; it was so ingrained in me to keep 'the secret' that it never even occurred to me to tell her what my home life was like. Her house was a haven and we had it to ourselves most of the time, with the exception of Tarnia's older brother who would appear every now and then to grunt at us from under his long hair as he walked past to get food from the kitchen, then go back upstairs to lock himself in his room playing guitar, or whatever it is teenage boys do.

...

By my early teens I had become a very good rider. I entered horse shows all over Victoria. It was something I loved and was good at and it kept my head above water. When you're riding it's all about you and your horse; there's no one to rely on, but that connection of trust and love that you build is amazing. It made me feel like I could do anything; that with hard work and perseverance I could achieve anything and leave the rest behind. Mum loved the escape of the horses as well. And when we travelled to shows we'd get up at the crack of dawn, driving off into the countryside to have a quiet day away from normal life. There, no-one gave a toss about who we were or what we looked like; only what we were capable of. Most people knew who we were, but they didn't care about that stuff. That was unimportant in the horse world.

The smells of the horses and the hay, leather and hoof paint were soothing for me. Horse people came from all walks of life: we would come together on freezing cold days, drinking awful coffee and watery hot chocolate in plastic cups from the canteen ladies, while everyone else was still in bed. In summer the smells were mingled with horse sweat and fly spray and the drinks were cold. It was a constant, reliable escape in my tumultuous world.

...

As I entered my teenage years, far from being in a safe place from which to tackle the tricky business of becoming a woman, I was an anxious, angry, rebellious mess with a collection of horses and dogs in my corner, but a family in the grips of a private crisis.

At 13 I became acutely aware of the way my body was changing. I had become used to my body's strength and ability to help me ride or play sport but now it began to get in the way. In the space of one year I had gone from my first training bra to a double-D-cup sports bra. My hips developed and, suddenly, all my clothes felt wrong. My breasts got in the way of everything I loved to do: horse-riding, basketball, running, dancing, swimming. They just kept growing and growing! This becoming-a-woman thing was annoying, and it seemed that everyone was starting to notice. Boys would giggle and laugh if my bra strap showed and the girls were forever comparing bra sizes. No-one came close to mine.

Perhaps I wouldn't have felt these changes as keenly if I had been born into a different family. I'll never know: all I do know is that weight and health were an everyday part of our lives. My parents' livelihoods depended upon their appearance, so we kids had learned from an early age what constituted a 'good' body shape and a 'bad' body shape. Everything was said on the premise that it was important to take care of yourself, but the less-than-subtle subtext was 'thin is good, fat is bad'.

If Mum was feeling uncomfortable in her jeans, she would exist on protein shakes for a few days. She exercised occasionally and never explicitly spoke about herself or anyone else as 'fat', but we were always aware of her body-size maintenance.

Me (left), Mum, Skye and little Hanna in front, hanging out. This looks like a shot my Dad would have taken: he loved black-and-white photography and we had a dark room in the house where he developed all his own prints.

Research has linked an appearance-focused family culture (including parental commentary about weight/size) with increased disordered eating and body image dissatisfaction in daughters.

'Family influence on disordered eating: The role of body image dissatisfaction', Annette S Kluck, Psychology MS 2051, Texas Tech University, 2009

Although Mum's job was all about her body being a particular size and shape it was actually Dad who paid almost fanatical attention to his appearance. He ran like a maniac and ate like a child. Dad's two sisters were large women (by BMI standards they would have been considered obese) and he made no secret of his anxiety that their size might mean he was destined to inherit the same genetic shape. To this day, he still orders a child's meal for lunch, and has a hard time sitting down to eat a dinner that adults would consider normal. Despite all this, we never heard our parents use words like diet; they talked about eating right and exercising, rather than 'getting fat'. Snacks in our household were nuts and celery sticks drizzled with honey. That was normal. I was amazed that the neighbours' kids were allowed soft drinks and packets of chips every day in their lunch boxes... those things were strictly party foods at our place. If we were hungry, Mum always had baskets of fresh nuts at the end of the kitchen bench, with a nutcracker available. We could help ourselves until meal times.

...

When I was 14 the trouble at home became unbearable. I had decided that I wanted to get out into the world and make my own way. So, I arranged to take myself to meet with a model agency. I had been around film sets and modelling shoots since I was very small and I had even modelled alongside Mum in shoots that wanted a child to be a part of the campaign. Dad had begun working in the theatre when he was 14 and Mum started modelling at 16, so the way had been paved for me to make an early start. It also wasn't the first time I had shown my enterprising side. I already had a little business that involved buying horses that needed work, training them up and selling them on to girls my own age who were looking for great all-rounder horses and ponies. It helped me justify buying better horses for competition, or at least that's how I sold it to Mum. I'd shovel manure into old feed bags and sell them for one or two dollars a bag at the end of the driveway, and I bought old bridles and saddles that I would spend hours reconditioning with leather dye and oils rather than buy new gear. I also did my very best to win or place in every competition I entered so that I could earn a little prize money for the kitty. I'm not sure how profitable it was really, but I think Mum loved that I tried to be considerate of the costs involved, because horse-riding is an expensive sport.

...

When it came to the modelling agency, my grand plan was to waltz in and have them sign me on the spot. I reasoned that by 15 I would have enough money to get my own place and be travelling the world, just like Mum. Easy, right?

I made an appointment with an agency. Not with my mother's agency, because I didn't want anyone to know what I was up to. I wanted to be able to do it all on my own so that I could walk into the house grandly that evening and announce my independence.

From the moment I walked through the door of the agency I was conscious of my mistake. The photos on the walls were all of lean, athletic models. It was the 1980s and Elle Macpherson was Australia's poster girl and epitome of beauty. My body couldn't have been more different from 'The Body'. Kate Moss had just been discovered and the trend was turning towards what would become known as 'heroin chic'. The agents were hoping to see a younger version of my mum walk in, but even though I was dressed in one of Mum's nicest Country Road suits, I was all curves where she was straight lines. I was the shape of the 50s not the late 80s. They were polite, but I could clearly see the disappointment in their faces.

They did their best to avoid embarrassing me too much, by telling me to come back in a few years when 'my shape had settled down'. I wasn't going to be signed. Not only that, but it was the first time I realised that my life wasn't going to follow the same path as Mum and Dad's lives. I felt the rejection like a sickening punch. Far from celebrating the changes my young body was going through, it became a source of shame. I hated it; I didn't want my body to change at all, I was content with how I was. I didn't want these strange curves coming out of nowhere; it was as if suddenly I was in someone else's body. It felt freakish and wrong. I can remember looking up Marilyn Monroe's statistics in one of the many books I had about her and realising that I matched her exactly. It was my only moment of reassurance during this time, because I thought: *she's considered one of the great beauties of all time, so maybe I'm not such a freak.*

CHAPTER 3

It hadn't occurred to me until then that the dreams I had for my future could be halted by the shape of my body. It's not that I had tickets on myself, it was just that I grew up around the modelling business; it was part of my life. From the day I was born, my picture had been taken for magazines, and this continued throughout my childhood. I grew up on modelling and movie sets. I had naively assumed that I would, or at least could, follow in my parents' footsteps. The rejection was a huge blow to my confidence. I had pinned my hopes for a future outside my dysfunctional family on life as a model, only to realise that I was fundamentally wrong for modelling. This was a time in my life when I needed a boost, or the very least a glimpse towards a happier future, but instead my dreams shattered in front of my eyes.

Among Australian high school girls, research has found that approximately 75% chose an ideal figure which was thinner than their own.

'Reining in advertisers to curb Australia's body image distortion', Nives Zubcevic-Basic, published online at theconversation.com, 2012

Living the dream. Another glamorous 'perfect family' magazine shoot to celebrate Hanna's birth.

After this devastating realisation I turned my attention to the only other job that held any interest for me: being an agent. Mum's agents, Greg and Katrina, were the all-knowing, guiding and glamorous mentors of our daily world. They were like royalty to us kids. We had to be dressed up and on our best behaviour in their presence. They each sat behind a huge desk in the most beautifully decorated office. Greg was impeccably groomed with long, shiny, black hair and golden, flawless skin. He spoke languidly and enunciated words like 'darling' with a practised drawl. He had perfect, sparkling white teeth and a lilting laugh. As a small child I would always try to spy under his desk to see the colour of his socks, which were brightly hued, made of silk and always different. Katrina was his physical counterpoint. She had pale skin and long red hair and she exuded effortless and immaculate elegance. Together they were a force of nature. The walls of their offices were lined with headshots of all the beautiful models they represented; the phones were constantly ringing, and the rapid conversations were all about models and photoshoots. My heart would race with anxiety and excitement at being so close to so much beauty and power.

Our family life revolved around waiting for calls from 'the agent'. Each afternoon, between 4.30 and 5.30pm, we waited by the telephone hoping for it to ring and tell Mum or Dad what their job would be the next day. There were no mobile phones or even computers and emails in those days, so if you were a model or an actor, this was how you heard about work. If you missed that call, the job could go to someone else. These calls would set the tone in our household. Missing out on a role

Dad really wanted or having to re-audition... those weeks were the worst. However, if the agents rang with good news, it was party time!

When it came to party time my parents and their friends were in their element. Parties at ours involved as many of my parents' friends as possible. They were a big bunch of Australian creatives and entertainers: actors, producers, artists, composers, singers and models. The parties were epic events that often went on all night. Us kids up one end of the house, holed up in our playroom, while our parents were singing, playing piano, dancing and drinking down the other. We'd sneak out of our makeshift beds and laugh at them dancing and swimming naked in the pool. One of us would keep an eye on the adults while the rest of us would pinch drinks off the tables. I loved these parties because we were all in the same boat, we all understood each other, no-one stood out or thought anyone else was stuck up for being famous. It was our normal.

My greatest childhood friend, AJ, and I met as babies among the heady party scene of our famous parents. AJ's father was an actor and good friend of my dad. They had been close since their days together on set when they were both single. AJ's mum and my mum bonded quickly over their similar upbringings, the strangeness of the industry and, no doubt, their alcoholic husbands. Many of the wild parties our parents held were at AJ's house, where we would get as far away from the drinking adults as we could. We would take ourselves away from the ruckus the adults were making and disappear up to his room to watch endless replays of *The Young Ones* and listen to AJ play his music. AJ wanted to be a rock star when he grew up and

I was his biggest fan. We found solace with each other, probably because we faced the same issues of identity and sense of place. We both had the same secret, the same pain and fear, but together we were safe and loved. He was my calm, I was his rage. We were Yin and Yang. In balance only with each other. While I used cigarettes and alcohol to numb myself, AJ put his pain into music. The bond forged as children against a familiar enemy remains strong to this day. It's like the melody of his battered heart matched the beat of mine and we will always be there for each other.

...

The times when my sisters and I felt like we belonged were few and far between. In our neighbourhood the parents went to the same job in the same place every day and they knew where their next pay packet was coming from. They could plan for holidays and special treats. My parents never had that kind of certainty: sometimes we would have treats and sometimes we wouldn't. Sometimes they could pick us up from school and sometimes they couldn't. Dad worked away a lot on location. Mum's jobs ran over time, or she would get a last-minute booking. When Mum and Dad couldn't be there my sisters and I would head straight to our grandparents' house or to our next-door neighbours, the Morgans.

My grandparents lived close to our house and my sisters and I spent a lot of time there while we were growing up. To be honest, I never wanted to leave. When Dad was at his worst or on a bender Mum would take us over to Nana's for a few days until everything had settled down.

The Morgans lived down the road from us all through my childhood and, along with my grandparents, were a constant and steady influence in my world. Ginny and Johnny Morgan were like second parents to us and, because their kids were close in age to my sisters and me, they became our extended family. I loved being at the Morgans' house. Their lives seemed so safe and normal. They lived loud and messy and would have screaming matches about everything: whose turn it was to take the laundry upstairs; who ate all the chocolate; who should take the dog out for a walk. Dinner at the Morgans' was either meat and three veg or Johnny cooking up something on the barbecue. Everyone would be yelling, laughing, fighting and making up. I felt free to be myself when I was there. I could be a part of a normal family life where there was no threat of violence. It was nothing like at home where a wrong word could escalate into abuse in next to no time.

Ginny Morgan reminded me of my Nana. She was firm but kind. She wouldn't put up with any nonsense, but she was fair. She let us be boisterous kids but not naughty. She would wash your mouth out with soap if she heard you swear but was the first to give you a hug afterwards. I loved her.

Johnny Morgan was a sweet and gentle man. He introduced me to books and I credit him with kickstarting my love of reading. Johnny sold books for a publisher and always had something to read in his den. I would sneak in there and curl up on his old lounge chair with a book. My favourite novels to pull down off the shelf were always adventure stories, fantasies and of course, anything with a horse. I must have read *The Silver Brumby* series by Elyne Mitchell at least a dozen times.

I raced through Anna Sewell's *Black Beauty* and Enid Blyton's *The Magic Faraway Tree*. As I got older I read Anne Rice, Raymond E. Feist and Robin Hobb books because they took me to another world. Snug in Ginny and Johnny's den, with the sounds of a busy household in the background, I felt so safe and happy. I have so many fond textural memories from the Morgans' home: the soft, thick carpet; the glass cabinet full of special things such as porcelain dolls and precious ornaments; and 'the good room' that was only used for special occasions and only opened for special people. Ginny always looked out for me. She may not have understood everything that was going on at home but she knew Dad was a nasty drunk — she had sent him home several times over the years when he had become too much to handle — so she would always let me stay with her whenever I turned up.

The Morgans' home was as much a refuge as my grandparents' house. Whenever life felt too hard to handle, I would just turn up and let their normal life wash over me.

My maternal grandparents' house was much the same. Grandpa was the gentlest, kindest soul you could ever meet. His love and understanding was a strong and consistent force. He was the life of the party but never a show off. His energy and genuine interest in other people was magnetic. There was nothing false about that man. I can remember overhearing him on a work call once when I was young. He was a real estate agent, which might mean something different these days but back then it was regarded as a position of honour and one that he took very seriously. I could overhear him on the phone asking a prospective buyer a million questions: about their family life; the things they liked to do; and, of course, about their finances. He asked and listened before I heard him tell them that the home they had set their sights on had so many problems that he thought it would cost them too much money to fix. When he got off the phone I asked him why he had pointed out everything that was wrong with the property when he could easily have sold the house and made money from the sale? He told me simply that he needed to go to bed with a clear conscience. He said that he knew he wouldn't be able to sleep if he was worrying about them getting in too deep. I still think about what he told me that day. It is important to go to bed knowing that you have been honest and tried to do right by everyone. It's something I've tried to do my whole adult life.

Primary school mug shot.

Experiencing abuse in childhood or adolescence has been identified as a significant risk factor for poor mental health, poor attachment and connection to parents and family, and general adjustment problems.

Child Abuse and Mental Health factsheet, Australian Government Department of Health, published online at responseability.org, 2005

CHAPTER 4

I was a sad, angry, depressed and terrified teenager. Our family was going through big changes. Dad's alcoholism was taking over his life and my parents' marriage was disintegrating. The control and stability I was craving as a young woman seemed further away than ever.

I felt myself losing hope for the future, so I began to live life as close to the edge as I could. I started hanging out with a crowd of kids who had home lives very similar to mine, some worse. As a gang we would delve into Melbourne's different subcultures and scenes. I tried out being a Goth, a mod, even a rockabilly; it was all about losing myself in whatever felt right at the time. I wanted to test my limits. I had been used to shutting down my emotions for so long that for me to feel anything at all it had to be extreme. I would drink until I passed out or threw up. I'd get involved in any and every drama that was around or I'd create some if I couldn't find it: train surfing, shoplifting, cheating on boyfriends, sneaking into clubs, hanging around with people way too old for me, experimenting with different drugs. Nothing worked though: I could never create enough external chaos to ease the internal pain.

In these years, I stopped crying and didn't feel fear. Such useless emotions, I thought, none of them work... you get a shocking headache from crying, and the thing you were afraid of was never the thing you should really fear. Losing your temper did absolutely nothing except to make your heart hurt with the shame of words you didn't mean to say and that could now never be taken back.

When I was 14 Mum took my sisters and me to Queensland to visit her sister. Our young cousin had recently been diagnosed with leukaemia and Mum wanted to be near her sister for support. We hadn't been there long before we got a phone call from my Uncle Max in Melbourne to tell us they had found Dad at home and that he was desperately unwell. Uncle Max told us that Dad had passed out after days of binge drinking and he had no choice but to take him to hospital. Dad was in intensive care. The news hit my numb mind and bounced off. I didn't cry and I didn't feel any fear; my overwhelming feeling was that he was getting what he deserved. I remember thinking to myself, 'Well, you've dug your own grave'. Dad spent about two months in rehab in hospital after he regained consciousness. The doctor told him that he had been a whisker away from death and that one more drink would be the end of him. I don't remember many details about this time, but I do remember that it felt hectic, fever pitched, as people say. I was in neutral, burning fuel, while my disconnected life was decided for me by adults in crisis.

It turned out that this was an end, but not of Dad's life. This was when the drunken lunatic died. The belligerent and abusive dad that we had grown up with was finally gone. There would be no more nights where I waited, trembling in fear, for the sound of his car in the driveway; no more frantic moves to hide from his drunken wrath. I should have felt relieved that my Dad had finally decided to never pick up another drink, but my wounded young self felt nothing.

Following Dad's brush with death, Mum decided it would be good for our family to leave Melbourne. It was partly a move that meant she would be closer to her sister, but it was also a way of keeping Dad away from old friends and old temptations. It was to be a clean slate for us all. I would start school again where no-one knew me as a troubled and rebellious kid. Our family's hopes hung on the move to the warm climes of the Sunshine State, nearly 2000 kilometres from home.

CHAPTER 5

We moved to Queensland and bought a house close to the beach. I was an instant misfit. It didn't help that the current fashion phase I was going through was rockabilly. The Sunshine Coast in midsummer is no place for hoop skirts and creepers. It was so hot and humid that I could smell my own skin, perfume, shampoo. Things that had never been part of my consciousness before were clogging up my breathing and senses. The move was a total culture shock in every respect.

At home in Melbourne, I had felt like people were interested in my thoughts and feelings. My circle of friends talked about art and music. In Queensland it seemed like the prerequisite for friendship was how good you looked in a bikini. Days were dedicated to sunbaking on the beach and getting a perfect tan was the penultimate life goal, just one step away from marrying a surfer.

The first year was the worst. Dad was sober and we had never known him like this. He had taken to sobriety with a kind of evangelical fervour and wanted us all along for the ride. Dad wanted us to attend Al-Anon meetings, established for family and friends of recovering alcoholics, so that we could share our feelings about his recovery. After a lifetime of being told to keep the secrets of our home life we were suddenly being told to share with a group of strangers, which was confusing and unsettling. Was it a trick? Would he find out what we had said and use it against us later? The group wanted us to tell the truth, but the truth was we couldn't believe that Dad had truly changed. He had said, so many times before, that he wouldn't drink again, but he always did. We had no reason to trust that this time was going to be any different.

After a month of feeling like an outsider in a strange land, I refused to go to school. I'd had enough of being the odd one out. It wasn't just my clothing choices or that I was the new girl, I was so culturally different in every way and didn't fit in with the surfer/bikini babes crowd. I had stopped playing sport and started gaining weight. I was terribly self-conscious and had started to smoke heavily and drink alcohol whenever I could. At the age of 16, I found myself sitting in a bus stop with a bottle of Scotch, watching the empty road and listening to the sound of the waves crashing on the beach. Life felt hopeless, I didn't know where to turn and asked God for help. It wasn't the first time I'd pleaded with the universe, hoping for guidance from a higher power, and it wasn't the first time that no help came. I felt like I was totally alone.

Dad's new love affair was the motorbike, of course.
I was a young child when this was shot.

Despite Mum's hope that the move to tropical Queensland would result in warmer relations between her and Dad, it wasn't to be and before long they decided to separate. Dad's alcoholism and the emotional and physical abuse he had inflicted on our family had taken too heavy a toll on their marriage. Mum decided to move further north, to Noosa, and for some time my sisters and I floated between their two households. I remember it as a strange time of dislocation and futility. Those around me — including total strangers — seemed to think that I would get my life back on track if I lost weight. The advice came thick and fast: how a boy I liked would like me back, if I lost weight; I would have a better chance of getting a job, if I lost weight; I would be happier, smarter, more lovable, if I lost weight.

Some advice was intended to be helpful but, in some cases, it was downright abusive. Take, for example, the group of men who surrounded me on the street oinking at me, telling me I was a pig; or the man at a bar that turned to his mate and said, 'She's alright, just slap her thigh and catch the first wave in'; or the man at a cafe who turned to me as I stood waiting in line to buy my carrot cake and coffee and asked: 'Do you really think you need that?'

Sometimes the jibes were posed as gentle reminders from people who loved me, statements like: 'You know, you would be really attractive if you lost a few kilos', 'You have such a beautiful face', 'Why don't we join the gym together?', 'I found this great diet plan I thought you might like to do with me'. Some were accidental, like: 'Oh, I'm sorry, I didn't realise you were pregnant.' Endless, repetitive judgement.

At night I would dream about taking a knife and cutting off the offensive parts of my body. I would fantasise about being rid of the big chunks of flesh that I had to wear every day like a suit for everyone to see. I felt as if I was being swallowed by it. My little soul was stuck deep down inside a disgusting body that I couldn't, try as I might, do anything about.

Dieting seemed to make it worse, not better. Taking prescription drugs made me lose weight because they made me feel so nauseous, but taking the pills also made me feel scattered and weak — like drinking 15 coffees on an empty stomach. They were too foul to stay on for too long, and every time I stopped taking them I'd just get bigger and bigger. I tried smoking instead of eating, but all that did was increase my addiction and rob me of my fitness. I tried just eating soup for months and eating only one type of food, such as cabbage, rice cakes or grapefruit. I counted calories and exercised obsessively. I tried every meal-replacement shake on the market. Nothing worked because none of it was sustainable in the long term. The second I relaxed the rules my weight would jump back up, and then some, in response to starvation. My metabolism was grinding to a slow crawl in an effort to try and conserve energy. My mind was screaming 'failure' at me 24 hours a day.

I was in a space of self-loathing and loneliness. My confidence had been dealt blow after hefty blow and I was struggling to find a way forward. But there was a glimmer of hope inside my mind; a flicker of indignation that was trying to fight the mantra of worthlessness the world was throwing at me. Why should I be judged so harshly just because of the shape of my body? There was a tiny but persistent voice inside that was saying, 'You are more than this'.

Shaming those who are overweight fails to help them to slim down. Instead, highlighting their condition or discriminating against them in everyday life can cause them to put on more weight as they resort to comfort eating.

'Fat shaming "makes people eat more rather than less"', Gregory Walton and Edward Malnick, The Telegraph, 11 September 2014

• • •

95% of people who lose weight by dieting will regain it in 1–5 years. Since dieting, by definition, is a temporary food plan, it won't work in the long run.

'Why diets don't work… and what does', Meg Selig, Psychology Today blog, 21 October 2010

CHAPTER 6

When I was in my early teens, I bounced from one mad crush to the next. At the time I didn't see any pattern in my infatuations but looking back I can see that I was always falling towards the boys that I thought were 'normal'. The ones who were likely to have the stable, traditional family life that I thought I wanted. The objects of my teenage affections were all steady, dependable boys who did well at school and had a predictable home life.

I was nearly 16 when I lost my virginity. This was late in my group of friends. My crush at the time was a nice boy called Scott. I had been crazy about him for about a year but I was too wild for him and he kept his distance. One school holiday, Scott had a few cousins come to visit from Melbourne. They hung with our group of friends for a couple of weeks. One of them was very like Scott, but with a wilder side. He and I ended up hanging out together over the holidays and one night, after more than one too many drinks, I let my guard down and we had sex. There was nothing romantic about it, just two drunk kids on the beach who knew nothing about true intimacy. The following day I was racked with guilt. Even though I knew Scott and I would never work out, I still felt like I had cheated. Perhaps it was because I had cheated myself and my long-held belief that I should be with someone like Scott.

In my later teenage years I went through a stage of one-night stands. It was never with strangers and always with guys I knew. My reasoning was that I wouldn't get an STD or AIDS if it was someone I knew. It was flawed teenage logic, obviously, but the TV advertisements about AIDS back then were all about fear mongering. The grim reaper was running around on TV lopping the heads off anyone who was stupid enough to have sex with a stranger and this was happening at the time of my sexual awakening. As a result, I was petrified! I'm sure that this mixture of fear, insecurity and a disconnected loneliness meant that I sought out long-term relationships over quick-and-easy sexual encounters. It was a pattern that I continued to follow into my adult life.

...

I met my first long-term boyfriend, Steve, at a nightclub in Noosa. He was the head barman at the local club and I was 18 and hanging out with a party crowd. Steve had a kind smile and, because our crew were usually the last to leave the club, he would often sit down for a drink and a chat after the lights were turned on and everyone else was leaving. To the outside world we may have looked like an odd match. He was a soft-spoken, introverted guy and I had a reputation for being a gregarious, outspoken girl. But it worked for us — at least, it did at the start. Steve was kind and gentle and just what I felt I needed at that time in my life. He made me feel at ease and he was so funny; we could talk for hours about everything and anything and we trusted each other with our secrets. We were both damaged from childhood traumas and neither of us felt comfortable in the surfer-dude/bikini-babe set. I was looking for a sign that men could be decent and kind and Steve showed me that. As for what he saw in me, he told me he loved my all-or-nothing attitude because it helped to draw him out and make him braver in his own life. While we were together he began to explore his artistic talent and to paint. He was a beautiful artist and in the security of our relationship he began to open up.

When I was around 19 or 20, Steve and I moved from Noosa to the Gold Coast to be near my sister Skye, who had just had a baby, a darling girl she named Maddison. Skye was only just 18 years old and I thought I could be helpful if we were closer. I knew enough about babies to know that they are hard work. Maddison was a gift. She was the only pure thing we had ever known in our family and we all vowed silently to protect her from life's awfulness if we possibly could. We wanted her to always know, no matter what, that she was completely and utterly loved. Twenty-four years later, she's still the most precious part of my life and now lives and works alongside me.

Steve didn't settle into the move so easily. He had a hard time with the disruption to his routine. He had lived his entire life in one area, just as his parents and grandparents had before him. Steve didn't like change. He had never expressed to me

Just another magazine cover: as a child I thought it was perfectly normal to see my parents in the papers nearly every week.

any dreams to see the world or explore the endless opportunities of life. He was all about wanting a quiet, consistent and ordered life and even though there was a part of me that craved safety and stability, I wanted to take the world on — I wanted to dive right in. Following our move to the Gold Coast the cracks in our relationship began to show.

...

On a night not long after Christmas I came home from work and collapsed on the couch, totally exhausted from the day. For a while I had been suffering with a dull ache and pain in my stomach. I had been to see a doctor more than once and been told that the pain was nothing serious and would ease if I lost weight. However, on this night the pain was steadily increasing and eventually spiked to a level that I couldn't bear. There was a fierce stabbing in my side and when I made a move to stand up I began to bleed. It was like nothing I had ever experienced before. Blood was pouring from me as though I'd turned on a tap. In a panic I called the hospital and spoke to an emergency nurse who said it sounded like a miscarriage. There was a slight chance I could have been pregnant because we were not overly careful when we had sex, but I didn't think that was what it was because the dull pain had been constant for months now. I didn't think I was having a miscarriage, I felt like it was something different. The nurse told me to lie down and keep a towel handy. She said if the bleeding hadn't stopped by morning I was to go in.

The nurse's words didn't provide me with much comfort and the pain continued to be excruciating. I remained curled up in the foetal position until Steve got home. He climbed into bed next to me, spent from his night's work. I started to tell him what was going on and despite what I was describing to him he told me he was tired and I should just wait it out. Maybe he had become bored by my persistent complaints about the pain or maybe he believed in the doctors who had told us things would improve if I lost weight. Whatever his reasons for ignoring the situation, he swiftly went to sleep. I continued to lie there in the dark, twisted in agony. Eventually I decided it was too much so I got up and drove myself to hospital. I was immediately admitted and kept in for over a week so that surgeons could operate to save my left ovary and fallopian tube, both of which had been blown apart by a massive ruptured cyst.

Although it didn't happen right away, I knew after I was released from hospital that my relationship with Steve was over. When we went out for Valentine's Day dinner we hugged for a long time and both agreed that breaking up was for the best. I had loved him deeply, but he wasn't the right man for me. There was no animosity between us and we remained friends for a long time.

While my mind was at ease over the end of my relationship, a fire had been lit inside me that wasn't going to be extinguished so easily. Despite the number of times I had been belittled, teased, abused or shamed because of my weight, this was the first time my physical health had been directly compromised by discrimination. I felt truly enraged. I wanted to go back to the doctors I had been to see several times and scream at them for making me endure pain that could have been avoided.

Because I was overweight they didn't even bother to check me out properly and had let me go on and on for months and months in pain until eventually I nearly lost an ovary. I was livid, furious with adrenaline and I began to wonder how many other women like me had gone undiagnosed with illnesses that left them in constant pain or worse because a health professional couldn't see past their size.

Weight bias in health care is particularly troublesome because it discourages people at high risk of health problems from receiving medical care or discussing health concerns with their doctor. After visiting health-care professionals, obese patients report feeling disrespected, not being taken seriously, and having all of their medical problems attributed to their weight.

'I See Fat People', Carolyn C Ross, MD, MPH, published online at psychologytoday.com, 2013

CHAPTER 7

I recall a conversation I had with my mum not long after my breakup with Steve. 'Why can't people see me for who I am, not what I look like?' I despaired. I was a good person. I loved and cared for my sisters. I was a loyal friend. I loved to laugh and to dance and I was a hard worker. It just didn't seem fair.

Mum's response? That she loved me for who I was, but she didn't want me to miss out on a full life because there were more people in the world who would judge me on my appearance before they knew me as a person. I think it was a hard truth for her to tell and an even harder one for me to hear. I didn't want to believe her, but in her experience of the world she was absolutely accurate. Even Steve had told me I was fat and disgusting and reminded him of his mother sometimes. I didn't even flinch when he said it. I had put on around

20 kilograms since we started dating and didn't feel comfortable in my own skin, so I agreed, even though it shattered my heart into a million pieces and undermined everything about love I had wanted to believe in.

I was at a crossroad in my life. I wasn't sure what to do next, but I knew I had to get out of the Gold Coast. I needed to go somewhere bigger and busier where I could flex my mind. I needed to go back to the city where people got up and got going and possibilities were everywhere.

Instead, due to lack of finances and perhaps because the universe had a message for me, I ended up back on the Sunshine Coast, moving in with long-term friends, Ron and Julie. A few years earlier I had worked part-time at Ron and Julie's restaurant and we had become great mates, even though they were around 20 years older than me. Ron and Julie had never been able to have children of their own, which may have been why they took me under their wing. I was a fiery and unpredictable teenager, but they never judged me and were always there as a support. They were beautiful, salt-of-the-earth people and it was just like them to open their house to me when I told them about my circumstances. I loved them to bits and trusted that they loved me for me.

Sitting on Ron and Julie's back step, I shared my dreams and told them about all the fantastical things I wanted to do with my life. Even though I was broke and unemployed with barely enough money for a tank of petrol, they never once laughed at me or tried to put me off my dreams. Instead they talked me through the realities, always giving me hope. They were just the human tonic I needed at this time in my life.

Pony club days were my favourite days on earth and an escape from life at home. Like me, Skye loved horses. She just didn't like riding so much! She preferred patting them and giving them hugs.

When my sister Skye decided to take her modelling career back to the bright lights of Melbourne I decided the time was right for me to return also. Our younger sister, Hanna, wasn't far behind. Skye's modelling career began to take off in Melbourne. Skye had Mum's genetically blessed physique, which made her just what the agencies were looking for. It wasn't long before she was booked out all over the country on fashion shoots.

Although Skye was doing well in her career, it was a difficult time for the three of us. We all had different issues to deal with while we were trying to navigate a new life in the city we had moved away from years earlier. It wasn't easy to reignite childhood friendships that had been stalled by the move to Queensland. We were like the new kids at school again, trying to find our feet and get to steady ground.

I found work as a make-up artist for Guerlain. My income was nothing like the salary my sister was earning, but I had a gorgeous navy blue uniform with a pink and red scarf and the job took me to different department stores across the city, where I would give special customers facials and makeovers for functions and weddings. My favourite store was the now-defunct Georges in Melbourne's CBD. It was decked out like a palace full of beautiful things. I truly loved that job, not just because I was able to move around the city meeting new people, but because my weight was never an issue for anyone: it was all about my talent.

My confidence was growing now that I was back in the city. There was so much to do, see, hear and watch. I was never bored. For the first time in a long while I was full of hope. I was

People who have a higher body weight are vulnerable to stigma in employment, schools and colleges, health care settings, public accommodations, the mass media, and in interpersonal relationships with family and friends.

'Weight bias is a bigger problem than you may think, experts say', Jacqueline Howard, CNN online, 29 September 2016 making lots of new friends who didn't know me through my family, so my size was just what it was. No comparisons. I had the glorious freedom to just be me. The dynamism of the city was sparking an idea of what I wanted to be and do. And the more I thought about it, the more I began to realise that it was time to jump out of the frying pan into the roaring fire.

...

One morning I received a call from Mum to say she was coming to Melbourne to help a friend and agent, Greg Tyshing, start up a new division of his model agency. Greg wanted to see if it was worth expanding into the commercial market and I saw it as my chance. I had known Greg for years as a friend of the family: my sister Skye was signed with his agency and he had also employed a former model and one of Mum's good friends, Marlene, as an agent. I was familiar with the current agency and would often pop by to say hello to the team. Now that Mum was on board I made even more of an effort to be around and I vowed to make it my mission to be as indispensable as possible. Each day after I finished my make-up work I'd head straight to the agency to help with absolutely anything that needed doing. I was free labour, so no-one minded me hanging around. They piled me up with jobs and I loved every minute of it.

When Mum's work was done and she was ready to head home to Noosa I leapt at the chance to convince Greg that I could step into her shoes. I pitched myself hard, explaining all the things I had learnt from Mum and Dad over the years and everything I'd absorbed from functioning as an unpaid intern over the last few months. Plus, I reminded Greg, there was the bonus that I was cheap. I was even happy to work and earn money outside of normal work hours. When I look back now I think, 'Poor Greg, I must have worn him out with all the pleading'. Eventually he relented and I was hired.

I worked hard at Greg's agency, not just to repay his trust in me, but because I loved what I was doing. I was the first person in and the last person out of the office every day. There was always something to do, someone to call, something to learn, dreams to fulfil. Greg was a tough boss but a veritable encyclopedia of the industry, so I was always trying to listen in on what he was doing and saying. I was in heaven when I was at work.

CHAPTER 8

I worked hard and played hard during the years I was working for Greg. I was part of a circle of friends that included my sister Skye and other top models. The lifestyle was fast and wild. We would all be at the same industry functions and parties, sometimes just managing to duck home for a shower before heading straight in to the office in the morning. The young generation of media moguls and high flyers were on the social and business scene and when they came to Melbourne the parties were off the charts: hotel rooms full of socialites, models and millionaires.

Drugs were everywhere and out in the open. Silver serving trays with lines of powder (cocaine, speed, MDMA, whatever your poison) were brought out at parties and passed around. I was no stranger to drugs; they had been a part of my teenage experimental phases, but they had never really taken hold.

Perhaps I was 'lucky' that I couldn't afford a habit as there was a good chance cocaine would have become my drug of choice and eventually, my nemesis. Overall though, I didn't like the out-of-control feeling drugs gave me.

Having a ringside seat to the kind of chaotic excesses at these crazy parties was all I really needed to keep me off the Class As. I had no desire to stand out in a crowd of rich and beautiful people, so I would stay on the sidelines with my Champagne and watch the madness unfold. Those on acid and special K (ketamine) would be playing with a room full of invisible balloons or talking with imaginary people. Those on cocaine would be in frenzied conversations or dancing like maniacs. Clothes would come off, inhibitions were non-existent. The hotel-room parties and VIP areas were where the really crazy stuff happened, away from public eyes. There was an unspoken rule that whatever happened on those nights was a secret to all invited.

I was happy to join the party on the weekends, but I left that scene behind for the working week. I was committed to my job and in the short time I had been working as an agent I had already witnessed too many young models lose control of their lives once they were introduced to the party lifestyle.

I knew a model, who was also a friend, who became totally addicted to cocaine and speed. She entered into a vicious cycle of using stimulants to get high and Rohypnol to bring herself down enough to sleep. At every party she would end up naked and dancing, writhing around to her own internal drug-fuelled tune on a tabletop somewhere. There was no stopping her. I watched as her weight plummeted, along with her self-esteem.

BONNER FAMILY

• Tony and Nola with their three daughters Chelsea, Hanna and Skye.

work. She was runner-up in the Miss International Quest and for many years one of Melbourne's top models. Now she is returning to her career.

"I enjoy working and getting out for a few hours so, now that Hanna is a little older, I have the time for more modelling work," Nola says.

Tony's acting career began in the early Sixties, his role in the popular Australian television series, Skippy, shooting him to international stardom.

So, when production on Skippy folded, he headed off overseas, living in London for five years and working on three movies — one with Tony Curtis and Charles Bronson.

He also worked with beautiful English actress Susan George and former Miss Norway, Julie Ege.

But five years overseas was enough. Tony felt claustrophobic in the crowds of London and after making a movie in Africa decided to come home.

For the past 10 years, Tony has been consolidating his reputation as one of our finest actors, and for eight of these 10 years he and Nola have been working to maintain their happy marriage.

And they have succeeded, having been spared the usual rumors that circulate about showbusiness marriages.

"The low periods between work could be a strain on the family, but I don't let it become one," says the talented actor whose film credits include The Mango Tree, Inn Of The Damned and The Man From Snowy River.

The winner of one Penguin Award and two Sammys for Best Actor, Tony has also had an illustrious television career with lead roles in such productions as Marion, Swiss Family Robinson, Power Without Glory, End Of Summer, Cop Shop, Skyways, and more recently, Intimate Strangers.

Tony has been lucky. The periods "between jobs" have rarely lasted long and he looks upon these low times philosophically.

"Either there is no work around or my look is wrong for the period. But it never worries me because everything works on a cycle."

In the meantime Tony admits to still being very ambitious, wanting to continue to grow, not just as an actor, but as a person and a parent.

"I learn daily from my children. I learn patience, tolerance and other areas of respect. Now I'm learning about a child's mind and it is a joy."

Story: Tracey Mair
Pictures: Greg Noakes

NEW IDEA, 5/9/81 3

This was a standard press day at the Bonner household, depicting our perfect glamorous family. It was all smoke and mirrors.

Only 5% of women have the body type (tall, genetically thin, broad-shouldered, narrow-hipped, long-legged and usually small-breasted) seen in almost all advertising.

The Body Project: Facilitator Fact Sheet, published online at bodyprojectsupport.org

She became the butt of jokes and went from being on everyone's invitation list to the black list because her behaviour was so out of control. One night at a party in a suite at The Como hotel in the upmarket Melbourne suburb of South Yarra I saw the worst of this scene laid bare. Alcohol and drugs were all around us, but it was a relatively sedate party by our usual standards. Most of us were lying around on couches and beds or sitting in small groups on the plush carpet listening to music, when my model friend stood up and started a slow striptease in the bay window. It was surreal rather than sexy and nobody thought it was funny or in any way entertaining. I could see the look of discomfort and pity in people's eyes. She was so painfully thin, like a starving animal that needed rescuing. Her protruding bones made her dance seem so desperate. I found it deeply troubling and instantly sobering. I got up and left without saying goodbye to anyone.

In the quieter times, when I sat with my girls in cafés and lounge rooms, just talking, I became an unwitting insider to the world of a top fashion model or for those young socialites who wanted to be one. The longer I listened the more I realised it wasn't a pretty picture.

Models are considered narcissistic, which comes with negative connotations, but the truth about being a model is that it's a job that requires them to be that way — it's the first and fundamental job requirement. That said, the constant fixation on their bodies would often come at a high cost to their health, both mental and physical. Because models' bodies are their source of income there's little differentiation between work and private life. It's not like the more common working lives that most women lead: most of these women can leave their job at the end of the day but models are on 24-hour alert. Models don't know where or when their next job might be coming from, so they feel forced to maintain a kind of body-awareness vigilance that can put enormous strain on their health and general wellbeing.

It may seem hard to believe but I knew many 20-year-olds who were paying big money for cosmetic surgery to remove invisible faults from their flawless frames. Models would pass notes back and forth about which doctors would perform a certain type of operation or who would prescribe a particular type of diet drug they clearly didn't need. I found it horrifying.

Most of the models I knew lived in constant fear of gaining the weight that could ruin their career. I began noticing that healthy, glowing girls whom we had signed just a few months earlier were starting to come into the office for measurements with distinctive watery, red eyes, which told us they had been vomiting up their food. If the girls weren't purging their food but using cocaine and speed to keep their weight down, they lost their careers quickly. It's not possible to maintain that drug-driven lifestyle in any sensible way. These girls would become scatterbrained and washed out with limp hair and pallid, grey skin. Some of the other girls would take laxatives like essential daily vitamins to ensure any food they ate didn't stay in their systems long enough for them to absorb the calories. So many models did things like this and everyone in the industry knew it was happening. It was, and still is, an open secret in the business.

There are a handful of models who are able to maintain the required physique naturally, without resorting to drastic measures; however, the majority of models will succumb to extreme weight-loss or weight-maintaining tactics at some point in their career. These tactics include exercising in plastic wrap, substituting a protein shake for every meal, even eating tissues or cotton balls to trick their stomachs into feeling full. These kinds of methods are so widespread that I'm wary of going into too much detail for fear that a young woman will read this and use it as a 'how to' for weight loss.

If we think about the statistic that only five per cent of women have a 'model body' and combine it with the number of working models there are in the world, then imagine what these women must be doing to themselves to maintain this extraordinary body type. And consider also, that they are expected to keep their battle with weight a secret.

Despite near impossible expectations there is an unspoken code that models never tell their agent if they are struggling to maintain the required weight. To admit that normal human hunger had won was to admit that you had no self-control. It showed that you didn't really want it badly enough. Through my sister Skye I had been allowed into the normally private world of a model, so girls would break the strict code of confidentiality in my presence and would talk openly to me about the stresses and strain of the business from their perspectives. It was not only heartbreaking to hear, I also felt some responsibility because I worked in the industry that held these women to near-impossible ideals. I knew the people I worked with at the agency were good people. Yes, they were agents, but they were also human. Unfortunately, not all agents are the same and in many cases all they see is the money and the work. If a model can't fit into the sample sizes provided by the designers then she won't be booked for a shoot or a runway which means she can't make money. Simple. Some agents didn't see the impact on a model's health and wellbeing as something for them to worry about. Being a behind-the-scenes part of the industry, I felt complicit. I was only 22 and a junior agent and, though I knew something was fundamentally wrong with what was going on, I thought I had no power to change the way things were. I thought the ways of the industry were out of my control.

Listening to the stories of the young women who came through our agency became the starting point for my re-evaluation of body image. I thought that if these beautiful young models — who had everything that society told women they were supposed to have to be happy — were struggling with their identity and self-worth, what chance in hell did the rest of us have? All my life up to this point I had assumed that only overweight people like me struggled with body issues. But now I knew that was not true.

CHAPTER 9

After a couple of years of working at Greg's agency I had begun to feel much more comfortable with my body. Watching what all these beautiful, young women were doing to themselves to work in our industry made me feel better about choosing the steak and red wine. I wasn't going to put myself through those kinds of horrors just so that I could fit into a certain dress size.

Although I was beginning to feel more content in my own skin, I was having a tough time finding any fashion that fitted me and made me feel good. I had noticed a couple of ads for plus-sized women's clothing in magazines and I would ask myself why the plus-size women were always depicted in their mid-30s with conservative brunette hairstyles? Where were the models who were my age? Where were the cool, young women in their 20s? I was desperate for fashion options, but I couldn't find myself represented in any of the ads for the clothes that

Skye, Hanna and me on our first day back at school after the holidays.

would fit. I was young, fun and on trend, not a mum with three kids. There must be other young women out there like me who loved fashion and wanted to look and feel good in their clothes.

I had an idea. I went to my boss, Greg, and asked him to cut me a new deal. I was going to get some pictures taken for a model portfolio and I wanted the fashion desk to represent me as a plus-size model. If I booked any jobs, he could take those days out of my holiday leave. To my delight, Greg agreed to go along with my plan.

My parents were friends with Australian media and fashion icon Maggie Tabberer. Maggie ran an eponymous fashion label, Maggie T, for women size 12 and over; this made her the perfect first port of call for my fledgling concept. Maggie was brilliant and immediately agreed to let me have my choice of outfits from her range.

I put everything I had into that first photoshoot. There was no digital photography back then so starting a portfolio was an expensive undertaking. It cost me the equivalent of more than six weeks' wages to set everything up.

I asked one of our wonderful agency photographers, Andy Tavares, to shoot me. Andy's wife Kim, a hair and make-up artist and a curvy woman herself, thought it was a fantastic project, so she jumped on board. I had studied the handful of models who worked in the field and because most of the models I had seen had brown hair I dyed my hair brown as well, so I didn't look too different. On the day of the shoot I felt weirdly excited. We were going to do it just like any other model's portfolio. It wasn't about being a plus-size model: it was about being a model. We shot in Andy's studio, where the light was perfect and we blasted the sound system to set the mood. Both Andy and Kim treated me with the utmost respect and professionalism. They made me feel so beautiful. I'll be indebted to them both forever for that experience and I still treasure the photos we took that day.

As soon as my portfolio was ready Greg began sending out the images to anyone and everyone he could think of who might be looking to use a plus-size model. I started booking work almost immediately. One of my first call-outs was for a collection of stores called Chain Reaction. The owner, Maria, could see that there was a gap in the market and she really believed in a younger look, so she booked me straight away. There were teething issues; like the time the clothing samples we were sent for the shoot were the wrong size, so we had to cut the dress right up the back and hold it together with gaffer tape. But I didn't care who I flashed my bum to: I knew from my parents that you did whatever had to be done to get the shot.

It wasn't long before I felt confident enough to change my hair back to its natural blonde and cut it into a short, modern style. One of my favourite clients, Robyn from *My Size*, loved my edgy look and booked me for a shoot straight away. I remember that shoot distinctly because the photographer wanted me to sit in the second-floor window of a broken-down old barn. This might not sound so bad, except that the barn was full of spiders and rats and the only way I could get to the window was to climb a dusty old ladder. I have two great fears in life: spiders and heights. So, while it might not seem to some like too much of a big deal to sit in a second-floor barn window and dangle my legs off the edge looking serene and happy, it took all my strength and willpower not to scream and flail about swatting at spider webs. When I look at the photos today I can't believe I look so calm when inside I was terrified.

Over the next year modelling took me all over the country. I was booked for all the major runway shows, which was a lot of fun, not least because Mum and Skye were also booked for the same gigs. In those days we only used first names as models and I can remember Skye and me being told off by a producer at one of the shows for calling Mum, 'Mum'. She thought we were being rude and ageist because Mum was the oldest model on tour. She didn't realise we were related and that she actually was our mother. I still love telling that story.

Another shoot that sticks in my mind as being one of the best was an editorial for the now-defunct *SHE* magazine in Sydney. I had done plenty of catalogue shoots and runway events but to get a magazine editorial in those days as a plus-size model was unheard of and simply amazing. I was flown up to Sydney and put up in a swanky hotel in Darlinghurst. I felt like a superstar. The photographer was Walter Rambaldini who was considered one of the best photographers at the time, so I was incredibly excited. On the day of the shoot I turned up on set and let the hair and make-up team transform me into the most stunning editorial look. The garments were high fashion and so on trend and glamourous. I'd never been given such beautiful pieces to wear before. One of the skirts was worth a thousand dollars. It was all going perfectly until we realised that none of the shoes were in my size, they were all far too big. It would have been okay if they had been flat shoes but they were sky-high stilettos and my feet just kept sliding straight out. Of course, they were an essential component of the vision for the shoot so I just had to try. After a few unsuccessful attempts at moving and dancing the way I was being asked, Walter's frustration with the shoes boiled over and I started to cry. I bent over so nobody could see and took some deep breaths to gather myself. I began to see the insanity of what I was trying to do so I just flicked my hair back and stood up laughing. Walter snapped the shot and it was perfect. I love that photo because it reminds me that, no matter how hard a situation may seem, if you can pause for a moment, gather yourself and have a sense of humour, magic happens.

At about this time I felt like I had to decide between being an agent or being a model. It wasn't an easy decision to make because I loved my job as an agent; however, I knew that opportunities like the ones I was being given didn't come around very often. I chose to leave the agency. I took with me a wealth of knowledge about the industry and some great friendships. The people I had worked with at Greg's agency were great teachers and I still find myself using what I learnt there with the staff in my own agency 20 years later.

The next year of my life was a lot of fun. I was modelling a great deal, but I also made sure to have a part-time job. I'd seen my parents and many models live from shoot to shoot and I couldn't cope with that kind of financial uncertainty. I always wanted to make sure that my rent was covered and my bills were paid. I worked in women's fashion stores on weekends and in the evenings and any days I wasn't booked to shoot. I would put my hand up for all the shifts other staff members didn't want, like public holidays, Christmas and Easter. I had also met a guy through a friend and things were going well. We had moved in together and done all the things young couples do. We bought furniture and pot plants; we went on weekends away; we hosted dinner parties and family events; I even bought a puppy, my little Harry dog. Harry would become the light of my life for the next 18 years.

...

When I began modelling there were a few other size 14 and 16 models coming through and I often found myself on set with the same women. In the shots that required two models, known as double shots, it was me — 'the blonde' — and either Bec or Alice — 'the brunette'. Both Bec and Alice were popular with clients and would often be flown to Melbourne from Sydney for the shoots. We became great friends. Over time, one of the things we all noticed during our shoots was how much better we looked in our own clothes than we did once we were made up on set. Shoots like the one I did with Walter Rambaldini or the one I had set up to establish my portfolio were by no means the norm. As plus-size models the clothes we were usually asked to wear were shapeless and boring. We laughed about it, but in truth it was laugh or cry. We didn't feel like we were properly represented at all. We would sit down in hair and make-up and watch the 'straight-size' models get made up to look fresh and glamorous while we would be transformed into conservative, middle-aged women. The idea was to cover as much of our bodies as possible. We were draped in massive shirts and baggy pants. God forbid anyone saw a womanly curve or a waistline.

Even skivvies, which are made to be fitted, were given to us four sizes too big. The aim was to make our faces the focal point. I was enormously bothered by being a part of an industry that was telling women that they should cover their bodies if they were larger than a certain shape, but I also thought that it was important that we were out there — at least we were being represented in some way, which had to be better than not being represented at all.

It was a catch 22. I didn't think I was in any position to change the way things were: I was just the model, I had no power, and I hated that feeling most of all.

Competing in the Royal Melbourne show when I was 14 on my horse, Bohemian Rhapsody — paddock name: Chips! To be able to compete at this level I had to travel all over the state and win several championships during the season, so it was quite intense. I was lucky enough to qualify several years in a row.

69% of girls concurred that models found in magazines had a major influence on their concept of what a perfect body shape should look like.

'Media and Body Image', Joel Miller, AdMedia

CHAPTER 10

Since becoming sober Dad had been doing well. He had steady work running acting workshops around Australia and was appearing in guest roles on TV. We were in regular contact and we'd catch up for special events. One particularly special occasion was the Australian film and television awards night, the *TV Week* Logie Awards. Following Mum and Dad's divorce, Dad would always take one of my sisters or me as his date. I used to love watching it all on TV when I was young, so to go along in person was such a blast. The only issue for me was that there was never anything appropriate for me to wear that was in my size. Evening wear for plus-size women in those days was almost exclusively mother-of-the-bride style and there was no way I was going down that road. Instead, I decided to mix it up and wear a man's tuxedo cinched at the waist with a lace bra peeking out from underneath the jacket. I finished off the look with dark red lips. I was really happy with the way I looked and I felt like I had cleverly avoided walking the red carpet in an outfit more suited to a middle-aged woman at a wedding.

On the way to the ceremony we stopped to pick up actress Jacki Weaver and TV presenter Derryn Hinch, who were on the same table as us. Our table also included Australian TV legend Don Lane and his wife and at the next table were soapie sweethearts Jason Donovan and Kylie Minogue, who were at the height of their *Neighbours* fame at the time. It was a brilliant night: fun, light-hearted and easy. In fact, I had been having such a good time that I decided to go to the after party with a couple of friends. I arrived at the hotel to go up to the room and entered the lift with a group of people including an actor who had just won a Logie. I smiled and congratulated him on his win and reached up to give him a kiss on the cheek. He looked me up and down before turning to his mate to say, 'I hope there's a better sort where we are going.'

They all laughed. I was shocked and speechless for a moment, but then I went ice cold. I gave him a steely look, directly in the eyes and said: 'I know your type. You'll be over and done with in a year or two. You'd better enjoy your moment in the sun, mate. People like you, who don't look at who you're stepping on on the way up, have no-one to catch you when you're on the way down.' My quick assessment of his character turned out to be accurate. His career did fade quickly. No more Logies nights for him!

CHAPTER 11

The more I worked in fashion, the more I understood what women over a certain dress size were up against. I had always railed against what I thought was a stupid argument that fashion magazines could only use size 8 models because that was the sample size that the clothes came in. After I had worked as a size 16 fit model for Myer I understood more about how the industry operated and began to appreciate what it took to create what is known as a 'block'. This is when designers and manufacturers determine a sample size at its smallest and then grade each size up from there incrementally. It takes hours and hours of fittings just to achieve the first size. The fittings I had at Myer involved meetings with the designers, quality controllers and heads of departments. In each meeting there would be an enormous amount of time spent pinching out and picking up tiny adjustments in the clothing to make them exactly right.

I was learning a great deal about the fashion industry from modelling and from my job at the time as visual merchandising manager for label Charlie Brown. I had found out about the job through the fashion grapevine and I had immediately leapt at the opportunity. It was a great job with flexible hours around my modelling gigs. While working for Charlie Brown and her husband Danny Avidan I learned everything from pattern making and wholesaling through to buying and retailing. Looking behind the curtain of the process, from beginning to end, was infinitely fascinating to me. I loved everything about the work. What I didn't love, though, was the endless prejudice I continued to face because of my size. In my role I had successfully and significantly increased their sales, which pleased the normally prickly and demanding Danny. He had a reputation for being a hard man to please, but we had a solid working relationship. I thought that we had a mutual professional respect until one day when he casually remarked that 'I did a great job for a big girl'. What a ridiculous thing for him to say. As though being a curvy woman would somehow inhibit my fashion sense. It sounds outrageously rude, but unfortunately it was a misconception I faced every day.

Thankfully, for every ill-judged, ill-informed and unfairly predisposed person I had to deal with there was someone who saw me for more than my size. My work as a fit model for Myer introduced me to two of the coolest women I know, Alla Buinowicz and Melinda Dachs.

Alla was the head of Myer's women's wear and a plus-size woman herself, so she had a personal interest in making sure that the products were perfect. She also wanted them to be as fashion forward as possible. Alla was a force to be reckoned with. I had never met anyone with so much energy and passion. She was no-nonsense and didn't have any time for 'no can do' attitudes. I soaked up all that I could from her. She knew the customer because she *was* the customer; there was no guesswork. She was cool and fabulous, smart as a whip, and wanted on-trend fashion that she would be happy to wear herself. She was an inspiration.

Melinda was a buyer in the team. She had a totally different style from Alla's, but an equally contagious amount of energy and drive and the best laugh in the world. It was the kind of laugh that comes straight from the heart with honesty and total unselfconsciousness. These two women were smart, strong, sexy and curvy and they were nobody's fool. We formed an unbreakable bond as curvy women who lived and breathed fashion. I was, and still am, indebted to these wonderful women.

The last year of Dad's alcoholism, on my way to school. It's pretty clear how bad things were from this dark shot. I was right in the middle of teen hell at this stage. He went into rehab soon after.

CHAPTER 12

Of all the weird and wonderful situations I've found myself in, the following story has to rank as the most random and bizarre.

My close friend Pam, a remedial massage therapist and lecturer in myotherapy at RMIT (Royal Melbourne Institute of Technology), called me one day with a proposition. Would I like to take her place on a weekend massage retreat in the Victorian countryside? Massage, beautiful country surrounds, fresh air, an all-expenses-paid weekend away. Sounds amazing, I thought. I would be crazy not to take her up on the offer.

Pam gave me the number of another guest, Alan, who was driving up and we agreed to share the petrol. Alan and I set off, both in a state of happy anticipation. As we drove I began to notice that Alan appeared nervous. He started telling me that his wife had been to the same retreat the year before and he was here now so that he could learn how to reciprocate. I thought it sounded like a sweet thing for a couple to do for each other, to learn some massage therapy techniques to be used at home.

When we were about 10 minutes away from arriving at the retreat, Alan realised that I had a very different idea about the content of the course we were enrolled in. Alan broke it to me as delicately as possible. It wasn't just massage, he explained, but rather 'tantric' massage. Otherwise known as erotic massage. We would be learning how to stimulate our own and, to my horror, other people's erogenous zones.

I immediately broke into a cold sweat. I could feel the panic rising. There was no way I was comfortable enough with my body to do something like this. If I had any idea that this was what I was getting into I would have run a mile to avoid it. It's true that I was getting better at accepting myself, but to be thrown into a room full of naked people who were learning how to massage each other's private parts was totally beyond my scope of reality.

As soon as the car stopped at our destination I jumped out and raced to the nearest phone. I rang Pam about 20 times, leaving her increasingly frantic messages. Then, when I didn't know who else to turn to, I rang Mum. I thought Mum would come and get me out of there. But do you know what she said? 'It will be good for you,' and she hung up.

I was terrified. Stuck in the middle of nowhere with 30 strangers, men and women, all learning about tantric sex. It was unbelievably confronting and I couldn't see any way out.

I was allocated a partner; her name was Lauren*. She was working as a prostitute but was here at the retreat to reconnect sexually with her husband. She was patient and kind with me and calmly said, 'Darling, there is nowhere I haven't been touched and nothing I haven't seen, so stick with me and I'll guide you through.'

We were separated into groups of men and women and went off together to learn about our bodies. The women were seated in front of a satin and velvet vagina and our teacher, who was naked from the waist down, had kindly pierced all the important parts of her own vagina so we could see and understand better. I sat as close to the exit door as possible, just in case I felt like sprinting for the hills.

On the second day we were in mixed groups. Again, divided into pairs. We were expected to touch our naked partner and stimulate them sexually. I couldn't bring myself to touch a strange man's penis in front of a room full of people, so Lauren stepped in and allowed me to 'hold the space' while she performed the movements. Although I tried as much as I could to be open-minded, I was nervous and uncomfortable and couldn't bring myself to participate fully. It took some time, but I slowly came to realise it was a safe space with lovely people. By the time it was over I walked out on a high. I felt light and free. Mum had been right, I did need this. I needed to connect with my body and my sexuality after so many years of internalising all the negative comments. The retreat gave me a simple message about self-love that I hadn't found anywhere else.

There is no denying I found the experience confronting, but it was the most liberating thing I have ever done for my body image and self-esteem. I owe Pam a debt of gratitude, but I've never trusted any of her weekend away offers after that.

CHAPTER 13

I had been working my modelling around other paying jobs for a while and, although it had been fun, I was missing my job at Greg's agency. I had enjoyed not having to think about anyone but myself, but I was getting restless and bored. Modelling was proving to be too slow for my racing brain and I also didn't like the feeling that I had no real control over anything. I was being booked as a young model to make older designs look fresher, but none of the fashions had changed to suit a younger woman. It wasn't unusual for me to go to set dressed in my own clothes and have the hair and make-up artists look at me after I changed into whatever I was modelling and tell me I had looked better when I walked in.

There came a time when I knew I needed to make a choice between being a model and becoming an agent. I loved modelling, but I also knew most models had a use-by date. It was a ruthless business to try and make a living in the long term. So, when I was offered a job heading up the Melbourne division of a Sydney-based creative agency I jumped at the chance. The agency represented some of the top photographers, fashion stylists and hair and make-up artists in the country and I was more than ready to be amid the frantic pace of it all again.

Things started well, and I was in my element. I was comfortable being surrounded by creative people because I'd grown up with them; photographers, actors, artists, and so on. My dad was obsessed with photography and we had had a darkroom in our house when I was growing up, so I knew a lot about composing images; everything about light and shade and capturing special moments. My work as a model and a model agent had refined my skills, and all the time I had spent training and working as a make-up artist made the job a perfect fit.

Unfortunately, though, it wasn't long before I could see that I wasn't going to get along with one of my bosses. They were a husband and wife team. I found her to be talented and hardworking, but he was a blowhard. All show and bravado. I had known quite a few people like him in my life and knew to be wary of them. Whenever he came down to Melbourne he would make me wait outside the office in the mornings while he escorted out the young model he had just spent the night with. He was a creep. I became increasingly uncomfortable keeping his dirty secrets from his wife. I respected her and enjoyed working with her and really wanted to tell her the truth. In the end, I quit. It was too heavy a weight on my conscience.

It was in the aftermath of that difficult and awkward work situation that I decided it was time to branch out on my own.

I was ready to start my own agency. I was 24 years old and blissfully naïve about how hard running a business could be. I wrote up a business plan with conservative figures and talked it over with friends and family. I ran it by colleagues in the business whom I trusted and who believed in me. It's true that I wanted their opinions, but I doubt any one of them could have stopped me if they had wanted to. I had my mind set and was ready to get going with my career. I wanted to be in total control of my own destiny.

I asked Dad if he would show his accountant a copy of my business plan. If his accountant thought my plan had merit, I asked Dad if he would be prepared to match my savings dollar for dollar. I don't think Dad even showed him the plan: he just gave me the money. Dad understood. He knew I wasn't one for an everyday office job or corporate rules and timelines. I remember his advice to me once when I had been offered a corporate position that paid extremely well; he said, 'Bucky,' (his nickname for me), 'you'd die under fluorescent lights with people who can't or won't think outside the box. Do what you love, stay creative and broke, you'll be much happier.'

He was right, and I felt grateful that I had a parent who understood and supported my dreams. I can't help thinking that many parents would encourage their kids to take the job with the money. Instead, with Dad's help and a grand total of $20,000, I was ready for the next chapter of my life.

This was also taken during the last year of Dad's drinking, around the time I was rejected by the modelling agency and all my life plans blew up in my face.

CHAPTER 14

I set up my new business office in the Melbourne suburb of South Yarra, a creative hub close to the CBD and a short walk from my home. The brand-new space overlooked a park and had beautiful natural light. It was perfect.

As I moved into my gorgeous new inner-city office I felt a sense of pride in how far I'd come. I was ready to jump into the business with both feet. No fear, just excitement.

It may have been that I was naive or it could just be an unlucky set of circumstances, but it wasn't long before my business took its first hit. It appeared that the sleazebag adulterer from my previous job was having a hard time accepting my resignation and new business. Such a hard time that he had decided to sue me.

I was shocked. I had always thought he was an awful person but I wasn't prepared for how vindictive he could be. The immediate effect of his lawsuit against me was that all the creatives who had given me verbal assurances that they would sign with me at the end of their contracts with him were now too nervous to make good on their promises. They wanted to wait until the result of the lawsuit was known. My former co-workers were polite if we bumped into each other, but they were generally stand-offish and reluctant to commit to any future relationship for fear they would lose their jobs.

I began to receive letters from lawyers saying nasty things about my character, work skills and business abilities. There were outright lies about my experience and my knowledge of the industry. They were trying to suggest that I had started work with the husband and wife team with no skills or contacts and that I had plotted to steal their contacts so that I could leave and start up on my own. It was horrible. I know now that the lawyers were just doing their job and I shouldn't have taken it personally, but it was my first experience with the legal system and I couldn't help but feel that it was a personal attack. I was hurt and angry. I couldn't believe he was flinging these accusations at me. The reason he hired me in the first place was precisely because of my experience and contacts. I was dumbfounded.

Lucky for me my close friend Nicki knew a lawyer and was able to put me in touch with him. His name was John and he was Nicki's brother-in-law. To my relief he agreed to take on my case. John quickly assessed what was going on and told me he was sure that the lawsuit was all about draining my resources and sending me broke. John's professional opinion was that there was no merit to the case, but that he was going to throw a great deal of money at it in an attempt to shut me down. Without John, I would have gone broke fighting the case. What my accuser didn't count on was my hatred of bullies. I was determined that he would not shut me down. It took two years of fighting: round upon round of facing up to threats and intimidation. There were days when I felt dead tired from the dual efforts of trying to manage my business and respond to all the ridiculous requests for paperwork I was being bombarded with. I dug deep, however, and found the strength to fight. I knew I was in the right. I also knew that I needed to clear my good name if I wanted a future in the industry. I hate bullies so I was never going to let a bully win.

John cleverly built in an early clause in our case that stated if we won, then our prosecutors were responsible for paying all my legal bills as well as their own. I think they underestimated my tenacity. I arranged a payment plan with John so that I could continue to fight. Finally, we got our court date and to my complete relief, the judge agreed with me. It was an unsubstantiated case. We had won. I cried with relief.

Although my fledgling business had taken a hefty body blow I was managing to keep my head above water. I had signed some amazing artists at the top of their game: hair and make-up artist Blanka Dudas and photographer Robert Earp were just two of the amazing professionals who came aboard. We were getting some great bookings and productions and my close friend Michelle had worked hard to set up a database of potential clients. At our first agency Christmas party the mood was positive and upbeat. Then, in March of the new year, the government introduced a new Goods and Services Tax

(GST). My clients suddenly stopped spending and budgets were frozen while accountants tried to understand the implication of the new tax on businesses. Invoices were held up and my cash flow stopped.

I desperately tried to hang on. I had fought so hard to get this far. My beautiful friend Michelle resigned before I was forced to fire her. I felt terrible. I tried modelling again to bring in some much-needed cash and I got a second job in a dress shop working nights and weekends. I closed the office and began working from home. I gave it everything.

CHAPTER 15

The stress and financial strain that my business was placing on my life took its heaviest toll on my romantic relationships. My boyfriend Todd and I had been together for more than four years. Like my ex, Steven, Todd had a quieter and more conservative personality than me. Todd liked living his life at a steady pace. He wanted stability, a home, three kids. Todd couldn't understand why I would want to throw all my savings and my time and effort into a business that might not work. He thought that crazy dreams were for other people, not for people like us. I had thought that I wanted stability and that being with Todd would bring me a sense of security and peace. In reality, I found the everyday normality stifling. The boundaries that he saw as comforting felt like a prison to me. I loved to see life as being full of endless possibilities, but he felt paralysing fear in the face of risk. The thing that terrified me the most was never giving it my all to achieve my goals. I never wanted to live a life of 'what ifs'.

Todd wanted me to quit my agency and get a normal job. I couldn't think of anything more depressing. The strain was eventually too much and we broke up. I was young and full of fire at the time and he wasn't. We managed to remain friends.

Four weeks after Todd and I broke up I found out that I was pregnant. The timing couldn't have been worse. I was broke, exhausted and single and now I was faced with a very difficult decision about my future and what I wanted it to look like. For me, the prospect of being a broke, single mother was something I just couldn't fathom at the age of 25. I called a few of my closest girlfriends and my mum to talk through my decision to have an abortion. I knew that it was the absolute right decision for me. One of the reasons I felt so sure was because the news that I was pregnant didn't give me any positive feelings whatsoever. My first thought was just, 'No'. As I mentally worked through the list of pros and cons with my friends and family it became totally clear to me that the cons outweighed the pros. I don't regret the choice I made. My life would have charted a completely different course if I had gone ahead with the pregnancy and I might never have been able to do the things I have done. It wasn't a decision made lightly but it was the right decision for me.

...

This was a difficult time in my life and I don't think I could have got through it the way I did without the love and support of my closest friends. I had a tight-knit group of

One of my first headshots as an adult, taken when I was seventeen. We were living in Noosa by this time and Mum was running a deportment and modelling school where I worked and taught beauty and make-up.

loyal companions around me and they provided endless encouragement, support and laughter. Our little gang was made up of Nicki and her husband George, introduced to me by my fabulously flamboyant friend and hair and make-up artist, Marc; as well as Simon, Pam and Cameron. Nicki was a top interior designer and has an incredible sense of personal style. I instantly fell in love with her twinkling blue eyes and raucous laugh. We were all slightly mad in our own ways and we all had a kind of creative wildness and cheeky sense of humour. We held epic dinner parties that went well into the wee hours of the following morning and crazy nights out on the town that often ended up dancing and singing in someone's lounge room. Despite being tested by time and distance our friendship has never wavered. We are devoted to each other still, 22 years later.

Around the time of my break-up with Todd, my baby sister came back to Melbourne for a visit. She had been living in the USA with her American boyfriend and, although we talked on the phone regularly, I hadn't actually laid eyes on Hanna in over a year. I can distinctly remember the day I went to pick her up from the airport. I was excited to see her again after all this time so I was early to the arrivals gate. I looked around enthusiastically, trying to pick her out of the crowd but I couldn't see her anywhere. I craned my neck to peer over the head of a blonde woman standing directly in front of me. Then the woman took off her glasses and smiled. I nearly fainted and felt the floor fall out from underneath me. Dread settled on my heart. I knew this look. The telltale signs of an eating disorder were plain to see in my sister's shrunken frame. My brain was

Numerous correlational and experimental studies have linked exposure to the thin ideal in mass media to body dissatisfaction, internalisation of the thin ideal, and disordered eating among women.

'Media and Eating Disorders', published online at nationaleatingdisorders.org scrambling to say all the right things and I was doing all I could to appear normal, but inside my mind was screaming, 'No, no, no'.

Over the weeks she stayed in Melbourne we saw each other regularly. I tried to subtly broach the subject of her eating habits and I watched her carefully for the familiar signs. She was reluctant to talk about it and all I could get out of her was that she believed that being skinny was the most important thing in her life. She believed that to be skinny was to be successful. She pointed to examples in the media. 'Look at the TV, the movies, the magazines,' she said. The message was everywhere. She didn't care that the cost of maintaining this lifestyle was her health. She couldn't see any other way. Reeling and desperate I tried to talk with her one night about my plus-size modelling. She looked me flat in the eyes and said she would rather be dead than look like me. A size 14. I wasn't offended. I just felt so incredibly sad for her. I didn't take it to heart, instead my heart broke for her. I don't think she meant to hurt me by talking to me this way, she was telling me what she truly believed. I had trouble arguing with her reasoning. She was right about the media bombarding us all with images of beautiful and almost exclusively thin women. I thought that we had been making headway as plus-size models, but we were really still tokenistic. We were by no means in demand with mainstream fashion or media.

My sister left Melbourne to go and stay with Mum in Queensland. I had filled Mum in as much as I could before she left, so she didn't get too much of a fright at the airport gate. It was the beginning of a long and arduous journey for our whole family. I couldn't change her life for her but seeing my sister in this state became another reason for me to try to change the way the world portrayed women. The problem was, I didn't know how I was going to do it.

My wonderful friendships helped me through the aftermath of my sister's visit and my break-up with Todd, but sadly it was not enough to stop the demise of my beloved business. I woke up one morning and realised I was done. I had to let the business go. It had become too much. I called in all my artists to tell them that I had to close. Most of them were understanding. They had seen how hard I had been fighting to keep the business alive. But it broke my heart to have to close a board full of so much talent and one that I was so very proud of. I felt like I had let them all down and I was devastated, disappointed and disgusted in myself.

In the matter of a month I had lost my relationship with Todd, my office, my savings and a baby. I curled up in bed with my little dog Harry, frozen in shame. I didn't get up for a week. Harry was the only reason I fought off feelings of suicide. I couldn't bear the thought of leaving him alone to starve. It was the first, but by no means the only, time that my dog has saved my broken heart.

CHAPTER 16

From the depths of my despair over losing my business, my sister Skye sent down salvation. Skye had fallen in love with a man who owned a creative agency in Sydney and she called to ask if I would consider making the trip north to talk to him about coming on board. It was a message from the universe. Skye's partner had not only offered to take over any of my artists in Melbourne who still needed new representation, but he was also willing to service the last bookings I had been unable to complete. I grabbed the lifeline with both hands.

At the time, the only mode of affordable transport I had was my old white hatchback Ford Laser with its distinctive baby-poo-coloured velvet interiors. I had purchased her for a measly $1500 after putting everything else I had into my business. I had even sold off my classic 1969 Mustang-style BMW that I'd never had the time or money to restore to its former glory.

My little Laser got me from A to B but boy did she have her quirks: I would need to kill the engine if we were stopped at traffic lights for too long because she would overheat; the driver's side window would drop into the car door if you wound it down too far; I had to use a pillow behind the backrest on the driver's side for the seat to stay upright; and she made a high-pitched squeal if she was pushed over 100 kilometres an hour. Despite all this, the old girl had always done me proud.

There was one time I remember meeting a client at the Crown Casino in Melbourne. While I would normally have parked where no-one would see me and my banged-up old car, on this day I couldn't find a parking space so I had no choice but to drive straight up to the front door and hurriedly throw my keys at the valet parking concierge. I was carrying a Louis Vuitton briefcase given to me by my good friend Marc and as I stepped out of my car the valet laughed and said, 'Your briefcase is worth more than that thing,' pointing to my Laser. 'Absolutely,' I agreed with a grin before running off through the doors. I made it to my meeting on time and I got the client. I was grateful to my trusty old girl.

When Skye called I had no choice but to hope that my Laser would get me as far as I needed to go. I needed her to carry me and my life from Melbourne to new pastures in Sydney. I packed her up with everything that I could squish inside, withdrew the last of the money from my credit card, grabbed the dog, said a prayer to whoever was listening and drove north. I had a new mantra for my life: it was 'just keep going'.

I arrived in Sydney in the middle of the night and was immediately intimidated. Sydney seemed so big and messy

Brunette! I dyed my hair brown to make myself look older when I started my career – hilarious! I'm definitely not a natural brunette.

compared to Melbourne. I drove around, disoriented, until I finally made it to my sister's apartment. The door was opened by her boyfriend Joe who immediately told me that he and Skye had broken up. Skye hadn't wanted to tell me before I got to Sydney in case I changed my mind about coming.

I made the decision to stay on but Sydney was a hard city for me to find my place in. The streets wound through the city like goat tracks. I would head off east and end up west. The one-way streets and the sheer volume of traffic made me feel lost and harassed every time I left the house or the office. It wasn't just the unfamiliar geography that I found bewildering, Sydneysiders liked to catch up at big parties and restaurants rather than dinner parties like the ones I was used to at home. People in Sydney were very protective of their personal space. My dad had a theory that Sydney locals were all about appearing outwardly successful, but that they lived modestly behind closed doors. He saw them driving fancy cars but living in tiny houses, which is why they didn't want to host visitors at home. I can't say if Dad's theory was correct, but Sydney definitely appeared to be bright and shiny.

The first people I made any connection with were fellow dog lovers. They would make conversation with me whenever I took my beloved Harry out each day. Without these small interactions it would have been an incredibly lonely time. Slowly but surely I began to make friends and eventually formed a little network of lovely, genuine people.

Although I had been living and working in Sydney for close to a year and had made some friends, I hadn't found my mojo. I had continued to model on and off, but plus-size models were not popular with the Sydney branch of the agency I was represented by. I had my job at the creative agency, through Skye's ex-boyfriend, and I was getting some regular modelling work, but it wasn't considered cool. There was one great agent in Sydney who believed in me and the potential for plus-size modelling, but she had decided to leave the agency and when she left she pulled me aside and told me frankly that she didn't think there would be anyone left who would be interested in pushing my career. She was right. I could see that they would book jobs for me but only when the phone rang. They were only prepared to do the bare minimum. I decided to switch agencies. I found a place that had just started to represent models who were size 14 and over. The problem was that they had never done it before so I effectively started managing myself.

I loved aspects of my 'real' job at the creative agency, but I couldn't ignore the growing dissatisfaction and guilt I was feeling being a part of an industry that was causing women and girls so much angst, self-doubt, body shame and critical comparison. I was getting increasingly angry. I continued to watch the parade of healthy, young models, fresh from country towns and outer suburbs, come through our doors, only to be turned around and sent out on jobs months later looking wasted and weak. Seeing these girls brought back all the fear I felt for my sister. I wanted to hug them all, ring their families and tell them to get out while they could. I was conflicted and confused and couldn't find a clear path forward.

I needed a break so I handed in my resignation. I kept up my modelling and got a job in Darlinghurst selling women's shoes. It was just the respite I needed. A holiday from my own head and space from the pressures of agency work. My boss, Sandy, was wonderful, a strong woman who taught me a great deal about business. Sandy schooled me in budgets and KPIs as well as how to close sales. It was like an internship in a way. Watching and learning things about balancing budgets, reaching sales goals, cost of sales and financial targets. I guess most casuals would have just walked in and sold shoes, but I'm always interested in how things work and why so I took the opportunity to learn as much as I could. The store manager at the shoe store, Olivia, also became a close friend, so close that I was a bridesmaid at her wedding in Ireland years later.

The shoe shop was in a traditional two-storey townhouse with the shop on the ground floor and the storeroom on the top floor. On our busiest days we would run up and down the stairs a hundred times. Sometimes we'd get dizzy from all the coming and going. I tell you, my butt has never been firmer in my life. The store was great and Darlinghurst was a fun suburb to work in. It was full of so many people from so many different walks of life. There were the Woollahra mums and the Bondi fashion set, the drag queens from Stonewall who came in because we stocked size 12 high heels and the office workers and corporates from the CBD who came to get their sensible block heels.

The pub a few doors up did half-price cocktails and karaoke on Thursday nights, so we would all head up after work for a drink. For me it was carefree time: my only responsibility was to hit my sales targets at the shoe shop and turn up on set for photoshoots for modelling gigs. Both of these things I did consistently. I may have bought too many pairs of shoes, but whether that was a downside is up for debate.

I let myself drift through life for a while. I dated, had fun, acted my age. I needed to gather my strength to find a new direction. When I felt ready to start again I bought myself a second-hand computer and began to research everything I could on plus-size models around the world.

My research was revelatory. In New York especially, plus-size models were a big deal and were really starting to make waves. Sophie Dahl had signed a major international campaign as the face and body of Yves Saint Laurent's Opium perfume, Emme was the first plus-size model to be named in *People* magazine's 50 Most Beautiful People, Kate Dillon was the first plus-size model to appear in US *Vogue* and Mia Tyler (Liv Tyler's younger sister) was featuring on MTV's *House of Style*. It felt to me like the beginning of a movement and I wanted to be right where the action was. I decided to do something I had put off earlier in my modelling career: I decided to move to New York. In the back of my mind I always thought that if my sister could see that beauty could be recognised and appreciated at any size then maybe she would get well. I had nothing to lose.

CHAPTER 17

Oh, New York — what a city! I fell instantly in love. Everything about it. Manhattan moved at the same speed as my brain, and I found it strangely comforting. Everywhere I looked there were pop culture references from my childhood and beyond: Woody Allen film sets; Broadway musicals; *Friends* and *Sex and the City* — everything felt familiar. One of the things I didn't expect from the city was the heat. New York in summer is like Southeast Asia without the beaches. It was so hot that I'd find myself gazing longingly at the gleaming Hudson River as I sweated through the city streets.

I had an amazing friend Kym, who was based in Manhattan and had offered to share her apartment with me until I found something more permanent. My friend and fellow model Alice was also heading over to NYC at the same time to meet with Ford modelling agency, so we travelled together. I met with several agencies in the first week and ended up signing with MSA Models (now called State Management). The model board I was on is now overseen by State Curve model industry matriarch, the amazing Susan Georget.

Although I had been signed to MSA, I still needed to kickstart some cash flow. I found a job in a classic New York Italian diner called Spaghetti Western in TriBeCa. The boss, Robbie, could easily have been an Italian restaurant owner straight out of central casting. He had a thick New York–Jersey drawl, gold chains dangling down the front of his one- too-many-buttons-undone shirt and a heavy weekend suntan. The interior of the restaurant was all dark wood, polished brass, plush red carpets and opaque glass partitions. I can still feel what it was like to walk in off the chaotic streets into this warm hub of wonderful smells, the garlic-rich pasta sauces bubbling away in the kitchen. The staff were a crew of people who had all come to New York for different reasons: we were a mishmash of cultures and backgrounds. My typical Aussie friendliness won me many friends among the staff because tips were significantly higher on the nights I was working. We were paid a base rate of approximately US$5.00 an hour, so tips were incredibly important. I would usually make between $150 to $200 a night in cash tips and would put my hand up for as many double shifts as possible. I needed to not only cover my expenses in New York, but I also needed to subsidise my apartment in Sydney (just in case I fell flat on my face in the Big Apple).

When I wasn't working or going to castings, my friend Alice and I would roam around the city, soaking it all in. We would catch the train out to the Hamptons, Coney Island or the Jersey

After I got rid of the brown hair, I decided to cut it all off anyway! This is one of the headshots from my first modelling portfolio.

Shore. There was so much to see and do that we would spend almost every spare moment sightseeing. One day, Alice and I decided to meet at New York's famous medieval art museum, The Met Cloisters. I planned my route on the subway but decided to get off early and walk through some of the neighbourhoods I was less familiar with. As soon I came up out of the subway, I knew I had made a big mistake.

The streets were not bustling with tourists or families or people shopping at their local grocery store. Instead there were groups of men standing huddled on street corners. I couldn't see any women or children. The atmosphere seemed menacing and I immediately felt vulnerable in my light summer top and shorts. I looked at my feet and cursed my flip flops. I should have worn trainers. My heart began to race, I could feel eyes on me. I began to walk down the street, pretending to look in shop windows. I felt a cold fear in my chest and an irresistible urge to get out of there as soon as possible. I dialled a random number on my mobile and began speaking loudly to no-one, while I walked swiftly to the next subway station.

The wait on the platform felt like two hours but was probably only two minutes. I couldn't get on the train fast enough when it arrived. I was shaking like a leaf. When I told everyone at the restaurant where I had been they freaked out before telling me that I had strayed into a neighbourhood controlled almost entirely by Mexican gangs. It was a no-go zone for anyone who wasn't invited.

Although I had moments of feeling like a fish out of water, for the most part New York was a bright and bold new world for me. As a plus-size model I was getting the opportunity to shoot with incredible professional photographers who appreciated curvy women. I was getting the kind of shots I had always wanted for my model portfolio. Young, strong, beautiful and sexy images that I still have to this day.

I was happy, life was good. I was feeling relaxed and peaceful, which should have meant the future would be bright; but there was a problem with my new-found happiness. I started to lose weight. This had happened to me before when I was at peace with myself. Not something that most plus-size women would consider a problem, but I had to maintain my size 14–16 figure to get work. Any size smaller than a US 10–12 was no man's land for a plus-size model.

The ridiculous hypocrisy of the industry had slapped me in the face again. To promote fashion for all women of all sizes the model needed to be a size 8 or smaller or a size 16 or larger. It was as though women between these two numbers didn't exist. Again, I was left questioning the morality of the industry. Why did fashion have to be so extremist?

CHAPTER 18

In Australia, the average woman is a size 14–16, in the UK and USA the average is 16. Nearly everyone else is between a dress size 10–14. Why then does the fashion world pitch their products to 20 per cent of the market and ignore the other 80 per cent? It's crazy. I started to realise that fashion sales and marketing had completely missed the mark.

Around the time I had begun to look at the statistics on women's average size and the ideal size promoted by the fashion and beauty industries, I began to loathe the label 'plus size'. I had never liked it much, but I was pragmatic about its use to describe a section of the fashion market. The thing I was beginning to understand, however, was that 'plus size' wasn't just a section of the market, it was the bloody market. We women, size 10 and over, make up the bulk of fashion buying power around the world. Was I the only one who recognised

The NPD Group estimated that 2016 spending on [US] women's plus-size clothing totalled $21.4 billion, equivalent to 17.5% of the women's apparel market that year ... These data points indicate that, as of 2016, the women's plus-size market ($21.4 billion) had reached less than half of its potential ($46 billion).

'A land grab is likely under way for the 46 billion womens plus size market opportunity', Deborah Weinswig, published online at forbes.com, July 2018 this? I was incensed. I kept thinking about the many young women whose lives I'd seen destroyed by a skewed and dangerous view of the world. Women were being sold an idea of body image that represented a tiny percentage of the actual market. It was an 'ideal' that was unattainable for almost everyone. I wasn't immediately sure what I could do about it, but I knew I needed to get to the bottom of why we were being shown the world this way.

Mum has always said that I have a strong sense of justice. And I charged at this topic like a bull. I wanted to find all the pieces to the puzzle. Why had I been told my whole life that my body size wasn't acceptable? Who were these people who showed us these lies about women's bodies every day? Why don't we women just tell them to piss off? I wanted to find out who was responsible for this insanity.

For decades, women's retail fashion has been led by emotionally manipulative advertising campaigns. In many cases it's based around a 'fear formula'. The fear within the market comes from the feeling that you don't fit in. It comes from being told you're not good enough if you don't look a certain way.

Most women do not look like the models used to promote fashion and beauty products and the upshot of this is that we have generations of women who feel like they will never match up to modern standards of beauty. So many women are desperately trying to emulate an unattainable image. The result? Several generations of women who have had their emotional, psychological and physical wellbeing compromised by the perpetuation of a lie.

If you want an insight into how advertising uses techniques

based on fear and manipulation, look no further than Matthew Weiner's iconic TV drama series, *Mad Men*. Set in the stylish 1960s, the show documents the birth of television and the advent of mass media through a thick haze of cigarette smoke. The first time I binge-watched the series I couldn't believe how accurate the representation of advertising was. It's all in there: the sexism, the outright lies, the twisting of truths and emotional manipulation to make people feel incomplete without a certain product. Take, for example, the episode about Lucky Strike cigarettes. In the program, health authorities have just announced that smoking provides an inherent and insidious risk to smokers' lives, yet the show's leading man, Don Draper, manages to turn a death sentence into lifestyle choice. He creates a campaign based around freedom of choice and anti-authoritarian rebellion that appeals to our intrinsic dislike of being told what to do. A clear manipulation of human nature. According to Don, instead of choosing to risk dying of cancer, you're a rebel, an individual, someone in control of their destiny.

There are striking parallels between this kind of marketing campaign and the beauty industry for women. If a woman can maintain an unnaturally thin physique, then she is to be admired. To hell with the health risks. Enter the diet and weight-loss industry. There's serious money to be made from making women feel inferior and inadequate.

Don Draper's way is only one way to sell a product. Recent advertising campaigns that feature images of real women, rather than models that fit a narrow and largely unattainable beauty standard, are becoming increasingly popular. The most

Terrified, but determined not to show it! Hanging out of a second-floor barn window with the spiders for the My Size shoot.

striking example of this kind of advertising is the Dove 'Real Beauty' campaign, launched in 2004. At the heart of Dove's advertising strategy was the decision to use women of all shapes and sizes, looking happy and healthy, instead of models. The market response was swift and overwhelmingly positive. Dove's sales figures increased by 700 per cent and it is widely regarded in the industry as one of the most groundbreaking and successful beauty campaigns of all time. Dove aren't the only ones to see the potential of this kind of advertising. Brands and retailers such as ASOS, lingerie retailer Aerie, skincare brand SK-II, British retailer Marks & Spencer and many more, have embraced the strategy of using realistic depictions of women and have seen their sales rise. But it's still not enough.

After a few months of working in NYC, I was booked for a shoot with *Glamour* magazine. It was a coveted job, even though it was a relatively small shoot. They had never booked a size 14 model, so my agent was thrilled. I knew it was an achievement and something of a breakthrough in the fashion world, but I couldn't help looking around at hair and make-up and thinking, 'This is such a tiny win in such a massive war.' The injustice of it all was burning inside me, but the feelings hadn't yet crystallised into a plan of action.

We are conditioned, they say, by the models we have around us, and historical churn in body image is designed to keep us in a state of perpetual dissatisfaction, driving the cosmetic, fashion and fitness industries.

'Your "ideal" body and why you want it',
Professor Tim Olds, published online at theconversation.com,
23 February 2016

CHAPTER 19

As far back as I can remember I've carried a heavy sadness. I've never known if it grew out of my home environment or if it was like a baton, handed down through my family's genetic code. Either way, I have always been a very empathetic and sensitive person. I'm susceptible to the smallest changes in the energy around me and I've always had a willingness to take on any pain if it means shielding the people I love. I think of myself as an optimistic pessimist, always looking for the bright side but never surprised by the dark. I used to think that if I took on the burdens of those I loved then I could save them from their pain. I've learned the hard way that people need to walk their own path. By stepping in with good intentions you run the risk of hindering someone's opportunity to learn and grow and you only end up exhausted and empty yourself.

When it came to my own burden to carry, I would feel its familiar weight first as fatigue and then as a whole-body heaviness. I understood the expression 'heavy heart' all too well, and from far too early an age. Dad called it the 'black dog' — though that was never a term that sat well with me because I find dogs to be the happiest of creatures — but, semantics aside, I knew what it felt like for the 'black dog' to settle in on my chest. I couldn't predict when the feeling would be about to hit. I would be travelling through life, enjoying myself and looking to the future with excitement when — 'wham!' — the heaviness would hit my body. I knew through watching Dad's struggle that the dog liked to chew on wounded hearts and if you didn't fight hard it could eat your soul.

I had been living in New York for a couple of months before I began to sense the darkness closing in. One day I woke and it felt like I was trying to move my body through mud. I was overwhelmed by lethargy yet couldn't get to sleep.

A couple of weeks before I felt the familiar weight of what I assumed was depression, I had experienced a disconcerting event. I realise now that this incident may have triggered my physical symptoms, but at the time I didn't know any better than to push through.

It was a regular day in the city, I was heading downtown to an appointment with my hairdresser. It was hot, stinking hot, and I was wearing light and loose clothing and little flat Chinese-style slipper slides. My plan was to come straight home to the air-conditioning after my appointment was over. I was halfway through having my hair washed when the power in the salon went down. Lights went out, the hair dryers went quiet,

A content analysis of weight-loss advertising in 2001 found that more than half of all advertising for weight-loss products made use of false, unsubstantiated claims. (Hobbs, 2006).

'Media & Eating Disorders', published online at nationaleatingdisorders.org

• • •

There is a strong desire among females to challenge existing beauty norms, with 71% of women and 67% of girls calling for the media to do a better job portraying women of diverse physical appearance, age, race, shape and size.

'New Dove Research Finds Beauty Pressures Up, and Women and Girls Calling for Change', published online by Dove at prnewswire.com, 21 June 2016 the music went off. Everyone stopped and stared at one another.

It wasn't long before we realised that the problem went beyond the shop. Staff and customers began making their way to the exits and that's when the fire alarm suddenly started. Everyone flooded the sidewalk and chaos erupted. It seemed that the entire borough of Manhattan had lost power. Over a million people who lived or worked in Manhattan were turned out onto the street as shops were shut down and businesses locked up. It had only been two short years since the trauma of 9/11 and New Yorkers were justifiably terrified. Whispers of a terrorist attack started swirling. Commuters were evacuated from subways, taxis were mobbed, buses were packed to the rafters. I lived on the opposite side of the city and when I checked my purse I had a measly total of $20 on me. I couldn't call anyone and I didn't know anyone who lived nearby. I remembered I had a friend staying in a hotel 20 blocks from where I was. It was the only place I could think of to go. So, I set off in my slippers in 110° heat. By the time I arrived it felt like I had been walking for hours and it was getting dark. The lobby of the hotel was a crowded mess of frightened people. Some were crying. I made my way to reception and asked if they could buzz my friend's room, but of course, they couldn't. No electricity meant no phones, no computers, no lift access and no way of checking if she was there or not. I was beginning to feel the panic. There was no room for me in this hot, sweaty lobby full of guests who couldn't get to their rooms.

The streets outside were getting more and more chaotic the longer the electricity was out. People's deepest fears about another terrorist attack began to feel more legitimate as each

Goofing around with my sisters, just before I moved to New York.

hour passed. I had no idea what to do, so I began to walk. I thought if I left now I would make it home by morning. I set off on foot. It was the strangest feeling to walk through New York City in total blackness. Not a single street light, but people everywhere. People began to light bonfires and I started to notice candles in windows. It was small comfort, though, as I knew that I was about to walk through a dangerous neighbourhood. I crossed the street to be nearer to an older couple who were headed in the same direction as me. I hurried to catch up and explained that I was on my own and would they mind if I walked with them? They were frightened but welcoming and immediately agreed.

We settled into an easy pace, eyes ahead, quiet and determined. My feet were filthy and covered in blisters. The temperature dropped and I started shivering. As we reached the most dangerous part of the notoriously dodgy neighbourhood, a four-wheel drive slowly pulled up alongside us and a man jumped out. By that stage I was almost too tired to feel afraid, but instead of threatening us, he immediately asked if we needed help. This wonderful man had driven all the way from Connecticut to help people stranded by the blackout. He drove all night, up and down Broadway, picking up petrified people and dropping them safe at home. I offered him my $20, but he wouldn't take it. Through my fog of fear, I saw the goodness. Basic human kindness had surprised and saved me. I climbed the eight flights of stairs in the pitch-black darkness and collapsed into bed.

The power didn't come back on until mid-morning. My phone lit up with calls from family and friends checking to see if I was safe. I watched the news to try to figure out what the hell had happened. It turned out to be one of the most massive power outages the USA had ever experienced.

The blackout shook me to my core and released a wave of pent up, confusing emotions. The darkness and the memories were coming.

...

I had once seen a psychologist who told me I'd managed to compartmentalise the different parts of my personality from an early age in order to endure my father's abuse and attempt to live a normal childhood. She thought that I suffered from Post-Traumatic Stress Disorder (PTSD) and had wanted to work with me to make me whole, join the parts into one. 'God no!' I thought. Better to keep all those feelings in boxes. I felt as though if I let them all out at once it would kill me.

One of my favourite sayings has always been, 'You don't need to step in a puddle to know it's wet.' This was how I felt about my childhood and my teenage years. There are big gaps in my memories. Whole years of my life that are hazy and as far as I am concerned it is for a bloody good reason.

I have feeble memories of a friend of my parents who was a part of the big crew of families we hung out with. He seemed to be always lurking and being inappropriately touchy. He frightened me as a child. His hands were always in places they shouldn't be. If he drove me anywhere, his hand would always find my knee. I can't recall any more detail than that or maybe, as I've hoped so many times, there is no more.

As unsettling as these memories and situations were, the

worst of the abuse I suffered was emotional and happened at home. I can't remember ever feeling safe at home when Dad was in town. And while I'm not trying to minimise what happened to Mum and my sisters and me, I also don't feel the need to go back into those darkest hours and dredge up old hurts. Not for me or for anyone. The father who caused us so much pain and suffering is dead to me. He is now a reformed man and has spent his life since becoming sober trying to heal, trying to give back and trying to make amends. I don't know if it will ever be enough. Sometimes just the tone of his voice will send me spiraling. When that happens, I try to focus on the effort he's making. When I don't like something he says, I walk away, or I call him out, instead of cowering in the corner. I have spent time blaming Dad for my pain, but it was ultimately a useless endeavor, so I let the bitterness and resentment go. I've accepted that my parents are just human beings. Flawed like the rest of us. They were shaped by their childhoods and they have had their own struggles in life.

I think that attempting to understanding my depressive feelings and the symptoms of PTSD I experienced has brought me closer to understanding and forgiving Dad. His father was abusive as well. Like a virus, these childhood traumas are passed forward. No-one ever showed Dad how to be a great father; his childhood had been about survival. He used alcohol to medicate himself, and for a long time it worked. Until it didn't. The alcohol let the demon out — it was always searching for a chink to crawl through. When Dad stopped feeding the demon, it went and sat weakly in a corner of his mind, unable to wreak havoc.

If I hadn't had the amazing people in my life giving me all the love, courage and support that they did, I might have ended up like Dad. I've come close several times; however, watching Dad fight the demon and win taught me resilience and empathy. I knew he was struggling to live with a dual personality and was never able to reconcile his drunken rages with his sober self. I'm sad that I missed the more traditional father–daughter connection with him while I was growing up, but I also know that no family is perfect and there is no point in dwelling on things that can't be changed. Today, Dad and I are more like friends or siblings: we're not ones for grand shows of physical affection, we're more likely to give each other a slap on the back like a couple of mates. I think he'd like to be closer now, but my body has a cellular memory that won't allow me to drop my guard that far. Despite our difficult shared past, Dad and I have found a way to be in each other's lives and to love and support each other's journeys. For this I'm grateful.

...

The symptoms of depression for me were like having a horrible house guest turn up and take over my home. I would have to give up my bed, share my wardrobe and my friends. She would pop in to work at the most inappropriate moments and interrupt my thought processes with stupid undermining questions. She enjoyed pointing out everything I was doing wrong and all the ways I could improve myself, while she'd stand in my kitchen drinking all my wine and smoking all my cigarettes. I hated her. I would scream at her in my mind, 'Get the fuck out!' I learned to starve her out: to not feed her

Clearly, people were not meant to be physically or sexually abused. Human beings are not equipped to understand abuse as it happens, not to feel the full force of their physiological response at the time. And they cannot, at that moment, find meaning in the experience of the abuse. Each of these important elements of accommodation can only happen later, in distinct stages.

'Post Traumatic Stress Disorder — Adult Survivors of Child Abuse', published online at adultsurvivors.blogspot.com, 25 August 2006

Big shoes to fill! The shot for SHE *magazine that Walter Rambaldini took when I was laughing. I love this memory.*

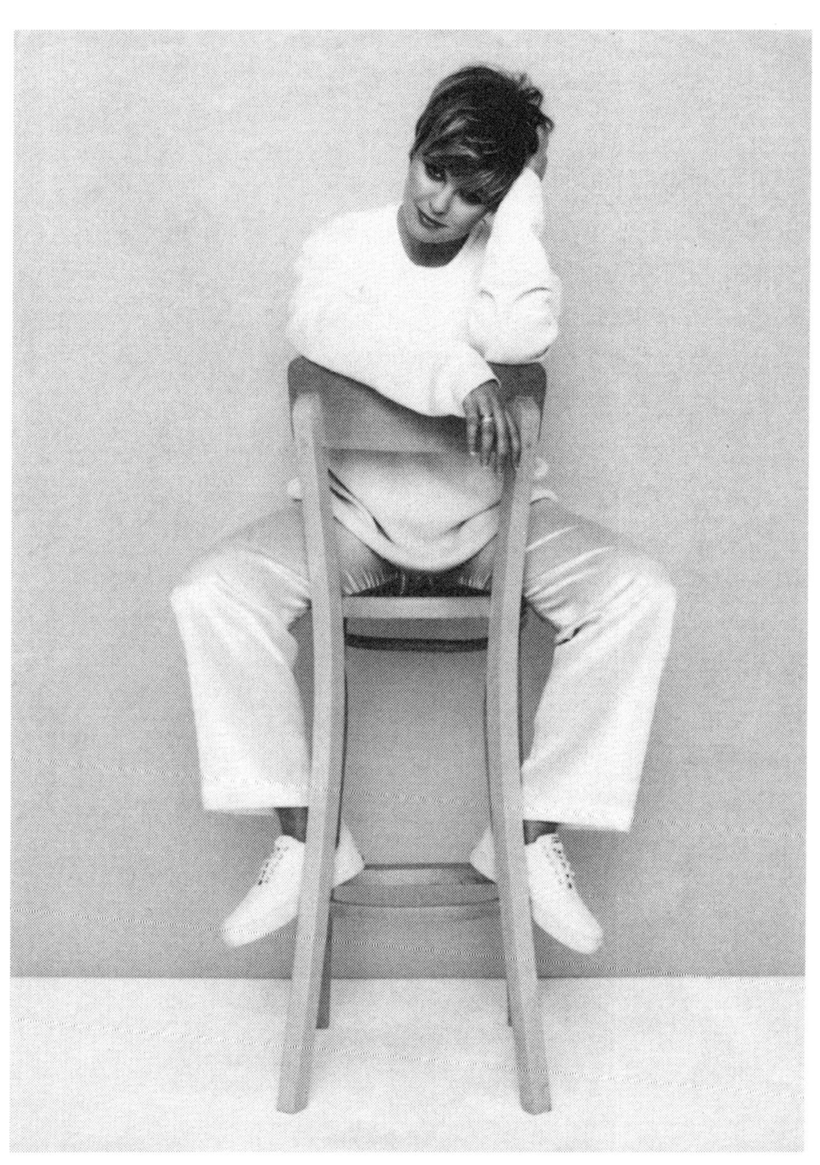

SHE *magazine again; part of the same great editorial shoot with Walter and stylist Fiona Milne.*

anything, not a scrap, because that was just the encouragement she was looking for. I would tell myself to look forward, get up, just keep getting up.

When I feel the earliest creeping feeling of depression, I make a point of setting my alarm earlier in the morning, so I have time to talk myself out of bed. I break my day up into tiny pieces instead of thinking about the whole day, which is too overwhelming. I talk to myself, tell myself to get up and get in the shower. Go and make a coffee. Get dressed in whatever I want. I give myself simple instructions: 'drive to the office'; 'answer the phone'; 'respond to that email'.

I try to think of it like it's the flu. It's going to hang around for a few days or a few weeks, but it will eventually go away. I try to keep moving. I make sure to walk every day, through the bush or along the water with my dog. I surround myself with things that make me smile: beautiful views, gorgeous flowers and happy dogs. I pull out all the little wonders of my world to counteract the negative. I find the wins and arm myself with them.

CHAPTER 20

At the age of 28, I decided it was time to leave New York. I had proven I could model there and I was now starting to miss my work as an agent. I was beginning to feel restless again. I rang my old boss in Sydney and asked how the agency was going. They were getting bigger, he said, and they were looking for someone to head up the hair and make-up division.

I flew home to Sydney with everything New York had taught me and all my experiences rolling around in the back of my mind. When I landed I jumped straight into work. Months went by and I was busy and happy. The odd well-paying modelling job still supplemented my income and my creative artists were doing well. When I finally settled into something of a routine, my thoughts would race back to the way the industry in New York treated the plus-size market. When I was working as a

When a patient is suffering from anorexia death can occur suddenly — even when someone is not severely underweight. This may result from abnormal heart rhythms or an imbalance of electrolytes — minerals such as sodium, potassium and calcium that maintain the balance of fluids in your body.

Other complications of anorexia include:

- Anaemia
- Heart problems, such as mitral-valve prolapse, abnormal heart rhythms or heart failure
- Bone loss (osteoporosis), increasing the risk of fractures
- Loss of muscle
- In females, absence of a period
- In males, decreased testosterone
- Gastrointestinal problems, such as constipation, bloating or nausea
- Electrolyte abnormalities, such as low blood potassium, sodium and chloride
- Kidney problems

If a person with anorexia becomes severely malnourished, every organ in the body can be damaged, including the brain, heart and kidneys. This damage may not be fully reversible, even when the anorexia is under control. In addition to the host of physical complications, people with anorexia also commonly have other mental health disorders as well.

They may include:

- Depression, anxiety and other mood disorders
- Personality disorders
- Obsessive-compulsive disorders
- Alcohol and substance misuse
- Self-injury, suicidal thoughts or suicide attempts

'Anorexia Nervosa', published online at mayoclinic.org, 20 February 2018

model I was making as much money as the 'straight' models and I was working with fantastic photographers and landing jobs in mainstream publications. In Australia, however, plus-size models were still being treated like outcasts. No-one had managed to crack the mainstream fashion market yet. It was also still bugging me that models like me were stuck trying to maintain a size 14 or 16 body to book work. Why did we have to work within such rigid confines? Why wouldn't brands book models who were inspirational and beautiful AND represented most of their customers?

Despite how incensed I had become about the treatment of the average-sized woman, it was the continuous parade of young, beautiful, 'straight' models through our agency doors that eventually galvanised my thinking. I distinctly remember sitting around a casting table in the studio one day and looking through the folios of the models we were meeting for an upcoming *Vogue* shoot. I had singled out a stunning girl who had a beautiful, healthy glow in all her pictures. We called her in — she had just come back from big shows on the European circuit — but when she walked through the door, I wanted to cry. She was a skeleton. The glow was gone, replaced with limp hair and grey skin. Worked to the bone, was all I could think.

You don't have to spend much time in the fashion industry to be exposed to unhealthy attitudes to food. I knew all about the kinds of things young models were doing to themselves to keep their weight down and their measurements at the required numbers. They told me their secrets and I could see it with my own eyes. It wasn't just what I could see; I had personally experienced the pressure and the shame of not having a body shape that was the 'right' size to be considered beautiful. I knew what this kind of pressure could do to young women. I knew what it had done to me. I saw so many young models go from healthy young women to shadows of their former selves. The saddest cases were the ones where I could see that the effort to be thin had become an obsession, but the absolute worst was when I could see they had become anorexic.

I knew anorexia. I knew it was a life-threatening and insidious disease, and I knew it personally because my youngest sister has suffered in its vice-like grip.

...

Knowing what I knew about eating disorders and the pressure on women to look a certain way had made me feel ashamed of the industry I was in. I knew we weren't personally responsible for each individual young woman's state, but we were complicit. We allowed it to happen and we perpetuated the lies. Every time a young woman like my sister buys a magazine or walks through a shopping centre and is bombarded by glamorised images of strikingly thin women, she's being told that's what she should look like. And it wasn't just my sister, it was all sisters.

My nana had always said to me, 'When you know better, you do better'. Shouldn't I have known better by now? I had seen so much damage done to young models by this point in my life. I'd seen how they progressed from 'It' girl for a minute to yesterday's news. I remember an agent colleague in New York telling me about the time he decided to quit because he felt as though he was trafficking young girls. His conscience wouldn't allow him to work in the industry any more. And, I might add, it was not a small agency he worked for, it remains one of the biggest and most successful agencies in the world — an agency I had desperately wanted to work for as a young agent.

The young women my colleague was dealing with were often from poor backgrounds looking for a way out or a way to help their families. What they weren't to know was that they had less than a five per cent chance of ever making modelling a financially viable career. Most of them would go on to become escorts at wealthy men's parties or worse: prostitutes at VIP clubs around the world; in debt from accommodation costs, flights and drug habits. They would be given just enough money to send a paltry amount home to their families, who would accept it, thinking their daughter/sister/cousin/niece must be living such a glamorous life.

I had experienced this kind of thing firsthand when I was a junior agent. I had sent a model to a reputable agency in China. We had used this agency before and had good experiences, but this model had a totally different experience. She was told as soon as she arrived that she had to lose weight and they would put her on a strict diet. The Chinese agency said nothing to us and she was too embarrassed to tell us once she was there. Over the next couple of months I started to notice that she wasn't herself. She avoided all my attempts to have a proper chat and was always 'just heading out' when I called. I was in regular contact with the agency who kept telling me she was going to castings but hadn't booked any good jobs yet and had not earned enough to cover her expenses. In the end I demanded they send her home when her contract period expired. When she came into my office to debrief — gaunt, grey and exhausted — she burst into tears and told me the whole story.

She had been too ashamed to tell me about what was going on, thinking there must be something wrong with her. At night she was sent to work in the agency's 'club', where models who weren't booking legitimate modelling jobs worked to cover their expenses. They would start out as waitresses and then move on to become a hostess. Then it was on to private parties and eventually, prostitution. All the while accumulating debt. It's a horrible cycle of abuse from beginning to end. Thank goodness I listened to my instincts and got her home. I'm sorry to say I've heard worse stories over the years and it's still a widely known part of the underground modelling business.

What was our industry all about? I was disillusioned and frustrated. I was watching my 'straight' model friends being 'aged out' of the market. These women in their late 20s were trying to compete for jobs with girls 10 years younger. These women tried to stave off aging by any means possible. Many resorted to invasive cosmetic surgeries and cosmetic procedures. They endured years of starvation, which caused medical problems that women in their 20s shouldn't ever be faced with. Bowel and intestinal issues, early onset arthritis, osteoporosis, crippled self-esteem. The list goes on.

And don't think that success as a model guarantees an easy ride. For many well-known and successful models, the years of being at the top often meant years of spending money like it was nothing. The problem with this lifestyle is that when they are no longer the flavour of the month the money stops.

So many of the high-income-earning models I knew ended up broke, renting a flat and using the fashion skills they had learnt over the years working in fashion sales. They ended up living week to week after earning what should have been enough money to invest and be comfortable for many years to come.

A young woman between the ages of 18–34 has a 7% chance of being as slim as a catwalk model and a 1% chance of being as thin as a supermodel. However, 69% of girls in one study said that magazine models influence their idea of the perfect body shape, and the pervasive acceptance of this unrealistic body type creates an impractical standard for the majority of women.

'Eating disorders: body image and advertising', published online at healthyplace.com, 30 May 2017

CHAPTER 21

On an evening out in Sydney, not long after returning from New York, I had an interesting and passionate discussion with my close friends Alice and Bec and a group of other models of all different sizes. We debated the absurdity and the hypocrisy of our industry. And, after way too many drinks and several rounds of pool, we agreed that no-one was taking us seriously; as models or as women.

We were all working models, but as plus-size women we were only ever portrayed as one-dimensional objects. And always in the same style of picture as well. 'Fat and happy' is what we secretly called it when we were on set. We would share a cheeky wink whenever one of us was put in yet another awful outfit designed to hide as much of our bodies as possible. We were not allowed be sexy, sultry or moody.

If the media was to be believed, then women over a size 10 were never any of these things.

The lingerie and nightwear shoots were the worst. The smaller girls were decked out in sexy, lacy outfits, whereas we were given enormous old-lady undies and strait-jacket-sized bras, even though we were all the same age. It was hard to ignore the less-than-subtle message that thin was beautiful and sexy and any woman over a certain size didn't deserve to feel sexy. She deserved to be covered up.

There were about five fashion companies in Australia at this time which catered to plus-size women. My fellow plus-size models and I loved working for them. They celebrated our bodies in the clothes and organised beautiful shoots that we wanted to be a part of. I don't find it surprising that these brands are still around today.

Bec, Alice and I were the go-to models for anything plus-sized, but we were also young, fun and sexy. Bec had no trouble attracting male attention when she wanted to. She could pick up just about any guy with one look. She happened to be married, but that didn't stop them following her around with puppy-dog eyes. Alice had men falling over in the street when they saw her. I'd seen men rubbernecking when she walked past. And as for me, it has never been easy for me to judge my own attractiveness, but I knew that I liked to feel sexy and didn't want to always be told that I had no right to feel that way. I think Bec, Alice and I were a lot happier in general than most models because we had less restrictions placed on our everyday lives. 'Straight' models would often look down on us as marginal models, but we felt terribly sorry for them, eating next to nothing to sustain a fleeting moment in the sun.

On our night out in Sydney we ended up in my apartment in Rose Bay, drinking wine and talking about how we would run our careers differently if we were in charge. The agency we were signed to didn't understand our point of view. Their website had a picture of the agency owner swinging a red umbrella with the words, 'the big girl who is light on her feet' splashed underneath. I wanted to die with embarrassment every time I looked at it. Was it any wonder fashion didn't take us seriously?

We talked well into the early hours of the morning and ended up coming back to one idea that kept rising above all the others. What would happen if I were to start my own agency and run it my way? There was only one way to find out.

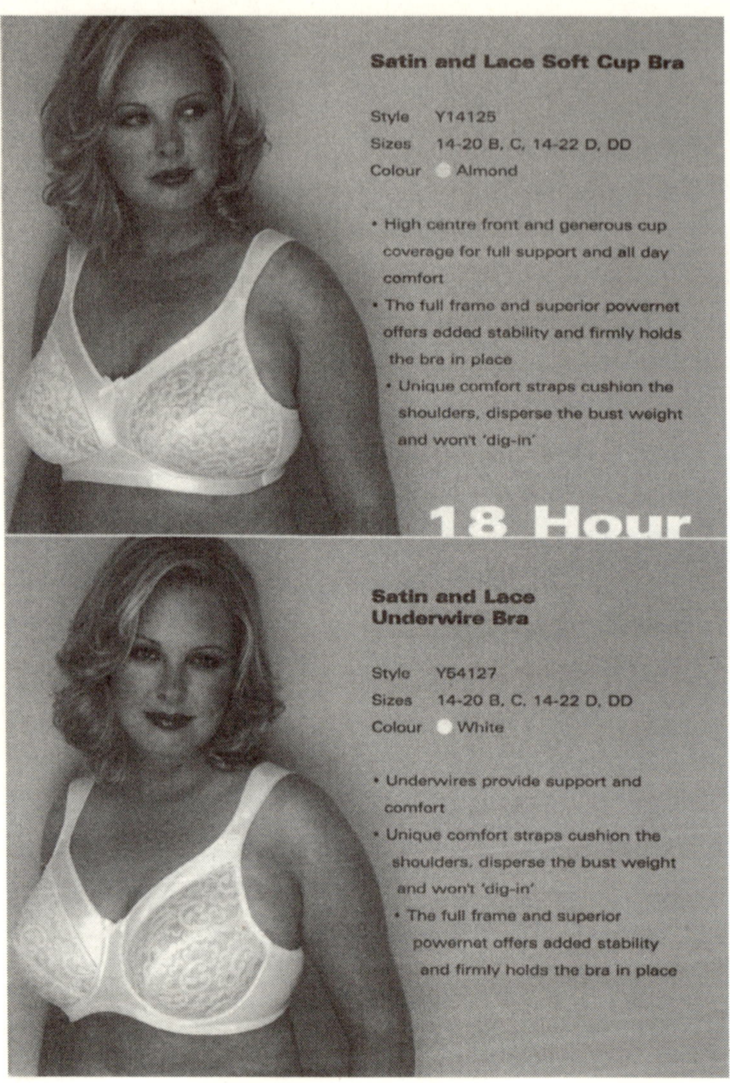

A campaign for Playtex lingerie in the early days of plus-size modelling. I was working with Tara Moss, who is so glamorous and was given beautiful lingerie to wear. Then my hair and make-up was done to try to make me look older and I got to wear the straightjacket bras! But it was a huge campaign that paid my rent for six months. I still book models for Playtex and they produce amazing modern and beautiful shoots now; we were all learning together then.

Research conducted by New York-based lingerie brand Adore Me revealed plus-size brunette models are likely to sell more underwear than slimmer blonde models.

The research was based on three TV adverts: one featuring blonde models, another brunette models and the third one a plus-size brunette model. The company then applied a common marketing strategy, known as A/B testing, to measure consumer buying habits and preferences.

The result was that the plus-size brunette model generated four times as many sales as the ad featuring blonde models.

'Revealed: plus-size models sell more lingerie than slim models', Linda Sharkey, *The Independent*, 23 March 2015

CHAPTER 22

I started building my new agency slowly. I had been burnt before when trying to set up and run my own business, so I was naturally cautious. In the beginning I was just managing Alice and Bec, and I kept my regular job at the creative agency. It wasn't going to be easy to juggle the workload: I needed to check my phone and emails for messages during tea breaks and lunchtimes and do all my marketing at night and on weekends when I got home from work.

I knew that I wouldn't earn enough in the beginning to make a living, but I would be free to do things my way. I could try out all the things I had always wanted to do differently in the industry. I wanted to protect my models. I never wanted to see the young women I was working with used up and thrown away, as I'd seen happen so many times before. I was determined to do more to protect them. I had plans to set up trust accounts and savings plans and provide investment advice so that when it was time for them to stop modelling they would have some financial security.

Most importantly, though, I wanted to change the way curvy women were perceived in the fashion and beauty industry and I knew I could do better than anything anyone was doing in that realm. I had wanted to change the world for my sister for so long and this was the best chance I had ever had to do that. I could use my skills, knowledge and experience for good. For the good of women like me and my sister and for all the women who want to be seen for who they are and what they contribute to the world. Not just for their size.

What I wanted was for every woman to feel worthy and deserving of beautiful things. I didn't want women like me to be portrayed as smiling cardboard cut-outs, grateful that we had been given anything at all to wear, let alone something that was fashionable.

Again, I sat down and worked out a business plan. I calculated how much I'd need to turn over to keep afloat and how much time I'd have to work outside the business to fund it. I tried to get a small business loan from the bank, but after two quick questions — 'What does your husband do?' and 'What do you own as collateral against the loan?' — they showed me the door.

I decided to start representing models where the 'straight' agencies left off. My smallest models would be a size 10 and I would go up to whatever size was healthy for the model. I wanted my models to be their natural healthy size, whatever that turned out to be. I wanted them to be able to gain or lose a few kilos without any judgment or fear of being let go from the agency. I wanted them to represent real women.

It was a radical concept. My parents and friends were dubious when I told them what I had planned. They didn't see that there was a market for that kind of model, but I had given up caring about what other people thought. I was comfortable with being the underdog. I didn't know if I'd ever make a living out of my idea, but I believed in what I was doing and at this stage in my career it felt good to be following my principles. It wasn't just about the money and, in any case, I had seen lots of miserable wealthy people in my life.

First things first, I had to come up with a name for my agency. I wanted something that sounded fresh and was free of any size connotations. Although it was my agency, I didn't want it to be about me, so an eponymous business name was off the table. I wanted something inclusive, something that would represent a team of beautiful, healthy people. I settled on *BELLA* models. 'Bella' is related to the Italian, Latin and Spanish words for beautiful and it was simple and strong. It said everything I wanted it to say about my brave and bold new venture.

With the name settled, I was off and running. My office was the bedroom of my run-down rented apartment in Rose Bay. I had a second-hand computer and a website designed for free by my close friend Rob. I had no idea what I was in for, but maybe that was a good thing. If everyone knew what life had in store for them then there would be times it would feel impossible to get out of bed with the weight of it.

CHAPTER 23

By day I worked in the creative agency and by night I busily researched everything I could about potential clients and market statistics. I needed to find just the right angle to pitch my business. I wanted clients to see that plus-size models were more than capable of pulling off fashion looks and shouldn't only be relegated to catalogues. I spent what little money I had left on arranging fashion shoots in the same style as the clients I was trying to attract. I wanted everything to be fresh and modern, just like what you would see on the pages of any high-fashion magazine or a national advertising campaign.

I was lucky to have been in the industry for long enough that I had access to the best photographers in the country, although I can't say they came cheap. It's true that sometimes photographers will shoot for free if you have an idea they're interested in or if the model being used is particularly amazing and they can go on to use the images in their portfolio. What I was asking for, though, was completely unheard of. No-one considered plus-size modelling to be a viable endeavour and most photographers couldn't see anything in it for them and their careers. Many even went so far as to tell me they thought I was mad. Thankfully, there was a small handful who understood what I was attempting to do, and they signed on for the ride.

I wish blessings forever to the incredibly talented photographers Simon Upton, who I had represented as a creative agent; Michelle Holden, who was one of my favourite photographers to work with as a model; and my good friend Henryk Lobaczewski, for agreeing to help me get going. I hired a talented junior stylist called Charlotte Stokes, who at the time worked at *Cosmopolitan* magazine. She is now the fashion director at *Grazia* magazine. For hair and make-up, I chose an up-and-coming artist, Charlie Kielty, who is now one of the most sought-after fashion and celebrity make-up artists in Australia. I've always trusted my eye for fantastic creative talent and watching each one of these amazing people succeed the way they have over the years has been one of my great professional joys.

My team was set so I went ahead and booked a superb studio that I knew had great light. This was going to be the first fashion shoot for my *BELLA* business, which meant it needed to represent everything I believed in. I wanted everything to be absolutely perfect.

I'll never forget that first shoot. I was finally witnessing my dreams come to life. To see what I had always believed was possible becoming a reality right before my eyes was exhilarating, nerve-wracking, thrilling and vindicating. The day passed in a blur of activity. My models were stunning, and the team of creative professionals was outstanding. I can remember standing on the sidelines and cheering them all on madly. I was so excited I must have shouted 'amazing' and 'gorgeous' and 'beautiful' thousands of times.

I may have been exhausted and broke, but that shoot gave me all the strength I needed to get me through the next two years. It was also all the proof I needed to show clients what was possible. You couldn't look at the images from that day and argue that it couldn't be done. This gave me my ammunition to strike at the issues I'd been railing against for so many years. These photos were going into battle with the media images women found themselves subjected to every day. The consistent portrayal of women in mass media as tall and incredibly thin was going to come under fire. For too long the depiction of women had been an unattainable and homogeneous one that doesn't reflect the majority. I believed it was time that the images we were seeing were ones that resonated as real. Wasn't it time the mirror started showing us the truth?

I used the photos we made on that first shoot and some pertinent research I had collected from the Australian Bureau of Statistics to create an email and online campaign that set out my goals. I laid it all out, plain and simple. The facts were, and still are, that the average woman is a size 14–16, weighs an average of 71 kilos and has an average height of 162cm. Where were these women in fashion, advertising and the entertainment industry? If these three industries were to be

This was what plus-size women were supposed to look like back then: as shapeless as possible and covered from head to toe. I was grateful for the work but so embarrassed that people would see me dressed like this.

believed, then most women didn't even exist. Any wonder we women get so angry and confused about where we're supposed to fit in the world.

Over the next few months my focus was on scouting for models. It became an obsession. Everywhere I went I kept my eyes out for beautiful girls and women who I thought had the potential to work. I found some of the most amazing fresh faces in the most random places. I found girls in supermarkets, clubs, pubs, beaches and the internet. When I wasn't scouting I was on the phone or email, pitching ideas and introducing the agency to anyone and everyone. I kept up the test shoots so that I always had new and current material to show clients. And you know what? It began to work. I may have been living on two-minute noodles at home, but on the professional front my hard work was starting to pay off. The business was picking up speed and needed me full time. It was time for me to quit my job at the creative agency and concentrate all my energy on *BELLA*.

Women drive 70–80% of all consumer purchasing, through a combination of their buying power and influence. Influence means that even when a woman isn't paying for something herself, she is often the influence or veto vote behind someone else's purchase.

'Top 10 things everyone should know about women consumers', Bridget Brennan, *Forbes*, 21 January 2015

CHAPTER 24

As *BELLA* gained momentum I noticed a shift in the way I was perceived by the mainstream fashion world. In fact, it wasn't so much a shift, but more like I'd fallen through a trapdoor. I had been prepared to be considered 'uncool' and I knew that what I was doing wasn't going to be celebrated by the entire fashion world, but the speed with which I was dropped from the scene made my head spin. Up until now I had been a part of a big group of friends and acquaintances in fashion and media; however, when *BELLA* kicked off and began to do well almost all my so-called friends and acquaintances disappeared. There was a desperate rush to disassociate themselves from what was being perceived as the 'fat' agency. Suddenly, I was off every invitation list. No more functions or events. I was even left off the list for social get-togethers.

There was one magazine editor in particular who seemed aggressively intent on bringing *BELLA* down. Every single time I generated some press for my models she would go on record to oppose our message. She vehemently argued that plus-size models had no place in high fashion and that she would never feature a plus-size model in her magazine. She believed that no-one wanted to see 'real' women in fashion. All I could think was that she should never say never. Especially to me.

For the next 10 years I didn't get a single invitation to a fashion industry event unless I was a 'plus-one' — no pun intended. If I did manage to get in, I would stand at the back of the room with the event crew and waitstaff because I wasn't allocated a seat. I remember going to an industry party at Pioneer Studios: it was one of their epic, four-storey events that everyone who was anyone was invited to. I mingled with everyone as I had always done, but when I mentioned what I was currently doing I got stonewalled. Industry insiders were either completely uninterested or shocked that I would consider giving up my job as a creative agent to work with 'fat girls'. By this stage, however, I couldn't have cared less. I had been to so many functions and parties in my career that I wasn't going to worry about missing out on a few. I didn't need more friends, all I needed was clients. Sure, being popular was a flattering feeling, but it was the work that really mattered to me now.

At the end of the first year of *BELLA*'s existence I was tired, but more fulfilled than I had been in years. It was a few days before Christmas and I decided that I should celebrate. I didn't have much money for luxuries like alcohol, but I wanted to mark the occasion. I popped down to my local bottle shop.

'Founded in 2006, Aerie is known for its affordable lingerie, lounge, and activewear, targeted towards 15- to 25-year-old female customers. In 2016, the brand made headlines when it became a forerunner of body-positive marketing... Based on Aerie's expansion plans, it's clear customers have responded positively to these campaign. The label is starting to pose a serious threat to lingerie giant Victoria's Secret, which continues to face criticism from customers and experts for its advertising approach, which relies on scantily clad women in racy ad campaigns. While Aerie expands its physical and digital footprints, ... Victoria's Secret announced plans to shutter 20 stores in response to poor sales. What's more, Victoria's Secret announced the discontinuation of its apparel and swimwear businesses in 2016, the latter of which continues to grow for Aerie. If Aerie's diversity-driven business strategy is winning out, perhaps struggling brands will get the hint that inclusivity is as important for business as it is for society.'

Sangeeta Singh-Kurtz, published online at Quartzy, 31 August 2018

I used to go there regularly before my money was eaten up by the business. I went to get my typical drop but realised I was $15 short on a $25 bottle of wine. I looked around and all I could see in my price range was a $5.00 cask. As I paid and was getting ready to leave, the cashier looked at me, smiled and said, 'Whoa, spending the big bucks tonight!' To his horror I burst into tears. I knew he was joking, but I was just so embarrassed and exhausted. Dreams don't come cheap and I was clinging on by my fingertips to realise them.

That night my girlfriend Sarah came over and we sat on the balcony of my flat until morning, talking, laughing and crying about the year I'd had. We drank the whole two-litre cask of wine to toast my first year in business — it tasted like gold to me.

...

A significant turning point for *BELLA* came when I signed my first new model. Tara came in to see me on the recommendation of a client. She was gorgeous, and I could immediately see which clients would love working with her. I signed her on the spot and organised her portfolio shoot. With the images fresh from the photographer I went straight to the art director for David Jones. Tara was instantly booked for one of the biggest campaigns in the country. She would soon appear in David Jones's catalogues and posters nationwide!

It wasn't until after she had landed the David Jones job that Tara admitted to me I had been her last stop. She had been to every other agency to try and get signed and every one of them told her she was too big or not the right shape or there was no

My first shoot in New York with photographer Roberto Ligresti, who has gone on to capture some of the world's most famous faces for fashion magazines and beauty campaigns. I brought my own wardrobe to the shoot and Roberto helped me choose the outfits. It was the first time I ever felt that a photographer had captured me properly.

market for her look. For me though, she was perfect and signing her was a game-changer. My little business had just booked a massive nationwide campaign and my beautiful Tara helped us live out our dream of representing body positivity through modelling. Since this first major booking, Tara has featured in thousands of fashion campaigns and magazines. She's one of my most loyal supporters and has acted as a wonderful role model for the young models coming through *BELLA*. She's an inspiration for Australian women in general.

As well as taking my message of body image positivity to the fashion world, I wanted just as much to see it received in the mainstream media. I couldn't think of a better place to start than commercial TV. My plan to break the diversity message to the mainstream media was centred around a competition to find Australia's next fresh-faced, plus-size supermodel. I had a client who ran a stylish clothing label who agreed to donate a full wardrobe as a prize for the winning contestant. I also knew friends in the media world from whom I could call in a few favours.

The first person I contacted was journalist and media personality Sonia Kruger. I knew Sonia from years of being in the same social circles and I knew she had recently begun work with the current affairs program *Today Tonight*. I pitched my idea for the competition to her and she immediately jumped on board. We set a date to hold the finals at the television studios. I received hundreds of submissions and whittled it down to 20 finalists. The winner would be announced by Sonia on *Today Tonight* and would receive not only a fabulous new wardrobe, but a contract with *BELLA*.

The competition unearthed several potential models, but there was a clear standout. A beautiful girl who, in the end, couldn't make it to the finals because of her work commitments. Her name was Abby Valdes. When I called to let her know she was a finalist she hadn't even realised that she had been entered because her friend had sent the photos in without her knowing. She was delighted to be selected and I was floored by her humility, as well as being in awe of her photos. She was sensational: glorious curves and glowing skin; long, dark, glossy hair and shining eyes. Even in the photos where she was goofing around, I could see that she could be a model at any size.

Although she didn't compete in the final of my modelling competition I knew I had to fly her up to Sydney to shoot images for her first portfolio. She was a star. She went from working full time as a finance broker and raising her young son as a single mother to modelling all over the world. In less than two years after I signed Abby, she called from a shoot in Spain in tears. I was instantly worried, but she quickly reassured me that they were happy tears. She was calling to thank me for giving her a start and for believing in her. She said, 'I was living hand to mouth and now I'm travelling the globe, doing what I love and being me.' I couldn't have been happier for her. I've had countless calls like these over the years and I never get tired of listening to the joyful voices. All I've ever wanted is to help women be themselves and be proud to be who they truly are.

Around the same time I found Abby I also uncovered one of my youngest signings, Sophie Sheppard. When I first laid eyes on Sophie it was in a tiny advert in the back pages of a magazine. She was only 16 years old. She looked so perfect that I thought her photo must have been a highly retouched stock image. Even if that was the case, I knew it was worth the effort to track her down. It took about 30 phone calls and 20 emails before I reached Sophie's mum Raelene in Perth. Sophie was undeniably beautiful, but she was also still in school. I have enormous respect for education and knew what a risk it was for a young girl to throw everything into a career in modelling. With that in mind, Sophie's parents and I agreed that she was to finish her schooling before she could model full time. Every model I've ever signed, I encourage to complete their schooling. That way, they have a fall-back plan if modelling doesn't work out.

Sophie wasn't a fan of having to wait. I think she felt we were being unreasonable and jeopardising her big break, but that's all academic now because she has taken the industry by storm, even modelling for *Vogue Italia*. She has been a full-time model with me for 12 years.

CHAPTER 25

BELLA had been in existence for around 18 months before I felt a seismic shift in the mainstream media's approach to women's body image. It started with a call from *Cosmopolitan* magazine's powerhouse editor, Mia Freedman. Mia wanted to increase the diversity of women's body types that were represented in her magazine. She didn't just want to include a token plus-size model every now and again, she wanted to ensure a consistent representation of diversity. She was going to include a size 14 model in every single issue.

...

This was a groundbreaking move in the fashion magazine world. I have always said to my models that every single shot that goes out into the world is important and has the potential to change a life. It may just be the smallest ad in a magazine that a woman will see that can make her feel better about herself. I knew the industry wasn't going to change overnight but we were getting closer to a tipping point. I believed there would be a time when it would be normal to see models of all sizes in advertising in every genre, everywhere. I also knew, being a size 14 myself, that seeing a picture of a fuller-sized woman in print made me feel valued and accepted. What Mia did was make every *Cosmopolitan* reader feel included. Don't believe me? The findings of Florida State University study back me up.

Researchers at Florida State wanted to understand the link between women's psychological health and the media's portrayal of women's body image. 'By measuring psychophysiological responses during image exposure, we were able to gain insights into the real-time cognitive and emotional responses that unfold when women are exposed to different-size media fashion models,' says Russell Clayton, Assistant Professor in the School of Communication. The researchers recruited a sample of college-age women, 18–25 years old, all of whom had said that they were dissatisfied with their own body image and wanted to be thinner. These women were then shown images of thin, average and plus-size fashion models on a screen. The participants' psychophysiological responses were recorded as they looked at the images. They were then asked questions about their body satisfaction and how much they compared themselves to the models on screen. The results showed very different responses to the thin and plus-size models. Here's the bit that I found interesting and made perfect sense to me: when thin models were shown on screen the women participants made more comparisons to their own bodies but remembered less about the model and came away with lower body satisfaction in themselves. Researchers acknowledged that this response could negatively affect the woman's psychological health. On the other hand, when participants were shown the images of average and plus-size models they made fewer comparisons to themselves, paid more attention and went on to say that they felt more satisfied with their own bodies. The upshot? 'We found overwhelmingly that there is a clear psychological advantage when the media shows more realistic body types than the traditional thin model,' summarised Professor Clayton (*Utilizing Self-Discrepancy Theory in Women's Cognitive and Emotional Processing of Models in the Media*, Florida State University).

...

The results of the Florida State study are a validation of what I have believed in my head for some time. I knew that *Cosmopolitan*'s editorial shoots featuring plus-size women could have a major positive impact on thousands of women. I also knew that Mia's decision would help me convince clients who were wary of using plus-size models because they would be able to see the success with their own eyes, in full colour in one of Australia's most popular women's magazines. Perhaps now they would be willing to take a risk themselves. It also meant that I could now spend some of my hard-earned pay on things other than photoshoots, because I could get content for marketing in a way I would never have been able to achieve on my limited budget. I went ahead and bought myself a $12 bottle of wine the night I heard from Mia.

Behind the scenes at a shoot with the creative team for Glamour *magazine, New York. This was the shoot that made me think about how much more I could do if I was behind a desk and not in front of the camera.*

...

From the outset of *BELLA*, I knew that promoting my message of body positivity would have the most impact in fashion editorials. The fashion magazines are where women go for inspiration, so this was where we needed to go next. I had *Vogue Australia* and *marie claire* firmly in my sights, but before I got there I had a breakthrough with Australia's highest selling magazine. *The Australian Women's Weekly*'s fashion director, Julie Russell, contacted me to say that she would be committing to three issues per year that would feature an eight-page fashion shoot with size 14–16 models: would I be interested in supplying models? It was a no-brainer. I loved Julie's styling and she was bringing on one of my favourite photographers of all time, David Gubert. I was over the moon to be involved. Our platform was steadily growing.

...

I knew that aiming for an editorial shoot in *Vogue* and *marie claire* was a complex undertaking. These publications had traditionally been opposed to the idea of curves in high fashion. I've had heated interactions with fashion magazine editors who tell me they think that plus-size models should never be accepted in the world of high fashion. They didn't think there would ever be a day when my models would grace the pages of the major magazines. Ever the rebel, all I could think when I heard opinions like this was, 'Watch this space'.

For Cosmopolitan editor Mia Freedman, reinvention has meant the introduction of a body-love policy that gives her magazine, she believes, a point of difference. Cosmo now has real women — in all shapes and sizes — on the pages of every issue and it has translated into a boost in interest.

'What Women Want', published online at theage.com.au, 13 October 2002

CHAPTER 26

During these years I was living a happy, single life. No-one to explain myself to. No-one complaining about my long working hours and lost weekends. No-one getting frustrated with me for forgetting about the shopping or missing dinner because I was working on a pitch. I could eat peanut butter on toast every night, wearing a face mask in my pyjamas. One word: freedom.

It's not that I wasn't interested in men or in sex, it was more that I had other priorities in my life than finding a partner. I had tried one-night stands, but it was never really my thing. Perhaps it was my personality or perhaps it was all those grim reaper ads for safe sex in the eighties. Whatever the reason, casual sex was just never something I went in for, and I wasn't searching for someone to make my life complete.

Perhaps if my attitude had been different I would have continued on in my single, merry way; though, as is often the case when you're not looking for something, it fell into my lap.

...

I had a call from a girlfriend who needed me to be her wingman for a night out. I wasn't in the mood for a big night, but didn't want to leave my mate stranded so I agreed to go along. It was the Sunday night of a long weekend and the city was heaving. In loyal wingman style, I pulled my unbrushed hair back into a ponytail and didn't bother with any make-up. I hoped I would be home on the sofa with my dog in an hour or two, but it was not to be. We'd been at the pub for a while when I decided to have a break from being the third wheel and wandered outside to light a cigarette. It was just as crowded outside, but I managed to spy a spare stool at the end of a very long table of guys. I asked if I could sit. They were celebrating a win in the local rugby final, so I chatted and laughed with them for a few minutes before I realised there was someone standing behind me. His name was Brett and I had stolen his seat while he was at the bar. He waved me down when I offered it back and went and grabbed an extra stool.

I've never been intimidated by talking to men. I love a laugh and I find the dynamic with men uncomplicated. Picking up that night was the furthest thing from my mind; I was just having fun being myself. After an hour of light banter, Brett turned to me and said, 'I'm going to marry you.' It wasn't perfect timing but when does life serve up that kind of synchronicity? Brett and I had a connection, we agreed, but

I had a European holiday booked with my friend Olivia. I had been planning it for a while and we were going away for a month. It was the first holiday I had been able to afford since opening the business. I didn't want any distracting attachments from back home. I had also been loving all the freedom I'd had lately. I was honest about all this with Brett and he said he understood completely. He said that my independence was one of the things he found most attractive about me.

...

When I got home from Europe, Brett was waiting. He settled into my life so easily. He was funny and clever, and I liked being around him. There was nothing not to like. But at the same time, I can't say there were fireworks. I remembered something my godmother told me once: 'Marry your best friend. The sex goes away, but the friendship lasts forever.' I thought maybe she was right. I had felt dizzying, crazy love before and it had never turned out well. Perhaps this was the real deal. There was a strong friendship developing and I felt understood and loved by Brett. I went along with all the sensible reasoning and let myself fall into a steady and comfortable relationship with a man I enjoyed spending time with. I did all this, but if I'm completely honest something deep down in my gut didn't feel right.

Brett and I moved into a house together after about six months of seeing each other. *BELLA* had been doing okay, but I was still living week to week and working out of my home. I was paying to have my cheques cashed quickly at the bank so that I could pay my bills on time. We weren't exactly living the high life, but that's how we rolled for a few years. Brett and

I hosted barbecues and drinks and went on weekends away with friends. I worked like a person possessed and built up my board to represent around 30 models. I started to tentatively believe that I might be getting to the top of the mountain, but as it turned out I couldn't see the mountain for the hill I was busy climbing.

Brett decided to start his own business. He had been working as a building manager in the city, a job which involved going from high-rise to high-rise making sure all the offices were cleaned and tradespeople organised. Brett thought the time was right for him to strike out on his own and I was behind him every step of the way. I lent him some start-up money for business cards and registrations and told him I'd pay all the bills at home until he found his feet.

He would come home in the evenings and tell me about all the meetings he had set up with big corporations. He told me that he needed to wine and dine the bigwigs to secure the contracts, so I lent him more money. When he started coming home with contracts, but needed cash upfront to buy the chemicals or other materials needed for the job, I lent him the money. Brett assured me that his contracts would be paid on completion. I was proud of him and proud that he was trying to start a business of his own. I knew all about what that felt like. He was up at the crack of dawn each morning. He would kiss me on the forehead when he left and when he came home late in the afternoon we'd pour ourselves a drink and share our work stories.

Around a year into our relationship we hosted a dinner party for a bunch of Brett's friends. We were all sitting around our

My second portfolio shoot in New York with the fabulous Roberto Ligresti. I was living in Marble Hill and caught the subway down on a sweltering summer day with a suitcase full of outfit options, many with the tags still on. I couldn't afford a fashion stylist, so I shopped all over Manhattan with my credit card and then, the next day, returned whatever I hadn't worn!

big outdoor table talking and laughing when one of his mates said, 'Chels, how can I get you to marry me?' I looked at him quizzically. He went on, 'Then you can cook and pay for me to have fun all day.' I thought he was joking, so I chided him, saying, 'Don't be mean. Brett works hard. I'm really proud of how well he's doing.' Well, their reaction was not one I could ever had predicted. Brett's mates practically fell off their chairs in amusement. 'Oh yeah,' they said through tears of laughter, 'working hard to catch up on his social life — it's not easy to get from café to pub.' I was dumbstruck.

I looked across at Brett: all the colour had drained from his face. I didn't know what to do other than just keep trying to be a good host while Brett's mates traded stories about his privileged life. None of them knew that I was completely in the dark when it came to his daily activities. The man I loved and trusted had lied to me. I wanted to lie down on the floor and cry, but I was too shocked, so instead I pressed autopilot.

...

When I look back now, I see that this was the first red flag trying to warn me that things were not as they seemed in my relationship. I probably should have left Brett that night, but we talked it through. He told me he had missed out on a couple of the early contracts he had bid on, but that he had more in the pipeline and he hoped that he would have made back the money before he had to say anything to me. He also said, 'It's so hard being with someone who's so driven and successful.' He confessed that he found it hard to be honest with me because I made him feel like such a loser. In hindsight, I can see that red flag waving madly, but at the time I was blind to it. Instead, I called Mum and asked for her advice. She had a suggestion. Her partner, Terry, was a project manager on major construction jobs and could offer Brett a job. It was great money, all accommodation and food paid for, the only catch was that he needed to commit to being stuck in a remote place for 10 days before he got four days off. Not a catch that was going to hold either of us back, we jumped at it.

CHAPTER 27

On an ordinary day in the midst of my life, I got a call from Dad. He was sick, very sick. A lingering cough that was initially thought to be pneumonia turned out to be a bacterial infection that had entered his lung and begun eating away at the tissue. He needed to be hospitalised quickly. The infection was fast-spreading and would kill him without medical intervention.

Now Dad is the most active person I know. He struggles to sit still for a minute so when we were told that he would need to be admitted to hospital for a month at the very least, but more likely many months, we knew it would be a test of both his mental and physical strength. I had recently taken up road cycling and every day I would ride the 45 kilometre round trip from my home to the hospital to bring him fresh food and real coffee. Then, when his condition finally improved enough for him to be discharged, I brought him home to live with me.

It was the first time in my adult life that we had spent an extended amount of time together. It wasn't easy. I experienced a lot of PTSD triggers — memories from my childhood and Dad's darkest days as an abusive alcoholic. In my rational mind I knew he wouldn't hurt me now, but the flashbacks hit me like physical blows. It took a few months and a lot of wine for me to stop feeling jittery in his presence and learn to recognise whether my reactions were based on past emotions or legitimate in the present.

I had to learn to look at situations with Dad in the third person. It wasn't an easy thing to do, but I'm pleased I did because the effort I put in to understanding my past and my present helped to heal my relationship with Dad. I'm grateful for the time we had together while he was sick. We were able to stitch up some old wounds that I didn't even realise were still bleeding.

...

About six months after I brought Dad home from hospital, Brett proposed. Things between us had been going well since he had started his new job at a power plant on Hamilton Island. We had a plan and a system where I would pay our bills at home while he saved all his pay so that we could rebuild financially and eventually buy our own home and maybe even start a family. This was something I had dreamed of all my life: a stable income, a few kids running around, my own home and everyone under my roof safe and happy. I knew that I didn't want to try and raise a child and be forced to choose between paying the electricity bills or buying nappies. If I was going to have children, then I wanted to know that I could give them a financially stable home. I wanted them to feel safe in all ways. Most of all, I never wanted to let them down. When Brett and I spoke about our plans for the future, I was excited.

We moved into a large, unrenovated (real estate code for old and run-down) Art Deco duplex with beautiful views over the harbour and a gorgeous, rambling back garden with a large studio down a garden path. It was close to Manly and close to public transport, which made it easier for me to run the business from home. I was riding my bike nearly every day and had even decided to train for triathlons, so my body was feeling fit and strong. Dad moved with us, into the studio at the back. Things had been tough for a while but it looked like life might be on the improve.

When it came to planning a wedding, I was adamant that we wouldn't spend an insane amount of money. Not when we were saving to buy a house. I had worked far too hard to be that frivolous with money. I put it to Brett that we should have a destination wedding: book a beautiful place in France for a week, where all our friends who wanted to could come and make it a group holiday–wedding–honeymoon all in one. So that's what we decided. Brett was working away so I organised the invitations and found the venue and worked out the food and music. We threw an engagement party in our back garden with fairy lights and a jazz band. I wore a gorgeous, green silk Fleur Wood dress that made me feel like a princess. Everything felt perfect.

CHAPTER 28

Dad had been healing well from his illness, but he was still too fragile to risk a long-haul flight to France. Instead he bought me my beautiful, champagne-coloured wedding dress. I wasn't sure that a big, beautiful wedding dress would be my thing, but Mum reminded me that the opportunity to wear a huge princess dress didn't come around too often and my mate Nicki had married in a pantsuit and always regretted it, so who was I to argue? Two days before we were due to leave the country for the wedding I ran around picking up everything we needed: suits for Brett and his groomsmen and all the things I thought I might need. I dropped in to pick up Brett's wedding ring from the jeweller and noticed while I was there that my ring was still waiting to be picked up and paid for. I wondered when Brett had planned to get it and even if he'd have time, but I didn't want it to be left behind, so I paid for both and headed off.

I hate this shot, but it illustrates just how awful the fashion was for us back then, and how unaccustomed the photographers were to shooting plus-size bodies. Could it be more unflattering, really?

It wasn't until we got on the plane that I noticed something wasn't right with Brett. He had started drinking in the airport lounge, but was really getting into it now we were in our seats. He was getting embarrassingly drunk. I was confused: his behaviour was out of character and he seemed bitter and angry. Once the steward had refused to serve him any more drinks, he turned to me with glassy, red-rimmed eyes and said, 'I don't have any money'.

I flew into a panic. 'What do you mean?' I said, totally blindsided. 'You should have tens of thousands of dollars saved by now.' He looked at me with a kind of blank resignation. 'How on earth are we going to pay for the wedding? You had all our savings! I've only put deposits down on everything!' I angrily whispered to him, trying to keep my emotions from getting the better of me. I was in shock. 'What do you mean you have no money? It's not possible.' I was close to tears. We sat in silence while I frantically ran through the last few months in my mind — everything we had said and done with each other. I couldn't see any hints or clues that he was draining our savings.

I was struggling to breathe. What the fuck was I going to tell the 40-odd guests we had flying halfway around the world to watch me get married to a man who had lied to me and betrayed me? I wanted to hit him in the head with the fire extinguisher by the exit. I wanted to scream. I felt like there was a howl of pain in my throat that was choking me. And, deep in the pit of my stomach there was a gnawing sense of shame at my stupidity for believing and trusting him when I had already been here once before. I kept repeating over and over in my head, 'Fool me once, shame on you; fool me twice, shame on me.' Brett had nothing more to say and fell into a drunken sleep. I looked out the window and wondered what I had done to deserve this.

...

If what I did next strikes you as crazy, try living it. My closest friends and family had flown, at great expense, to the other side of the world. Some with their children. To spend a week in a chateau in France for a wedding and a holiday. All I knew to do was to get on with it. For now, I needed to put the pain and disappointment in one of my airtight emotional boxes and pack it away for when we got home. Before that, though, I got drunk, very drunk.

We arrived in the Paris hotel where we were meeting a few friends who were flying in early. We had plans to roam the city together before we went out to the countryside. Brett went straight to our room and went to sleep. I wandered the streets and found a bar. I sat down and drank several glasses of red wine: it may have even been a bottle. I drank enough to make the weight of the disappointment and confusion disappear. Then I went for a facial and let them pamper and soothe me before I had to plaster on a smile the next day and pretend everything was okay.

Being in a big group kept Brett and me busy, so we didn't have the time or space to dwell on our dire financial situation. Brett had admitted to having $2000 left and I had a credit card and a sum of money that I was holding for tax. We could make it through the month at least.

Lies, betrayal and financial ruin aside, Brett and I and our friends and family had a ball that week. We saw beautiful things and we ate beautiful food and we laughed together. It was a week of magical experiences. Until the fourth day, when I got what we all laughingly referred to as 'le French flu'. We joked, but I felt like death warmed up. My heart was telling me it was the universe stepping in to stop me going through with the wedding, but I didn't listen. Like a stubborn mule, I powered through. The night before the wedding my friend Bec dosed me up on cold-and-flu tablets and helped me shower before rubbing fake tan all over my feverish body. Just as I was crawling into bed I had a call from a client in Australia who needed my help to book a campaign for Myer. Obviously, I couldn't turn down any earnings at that point, so when everyone was tucked up for the night I sat down in the chateau office, shivering with fever, talking through model options in the middle of the night. Working so I could pay for the wedding I was about to have, to a man whom I now knew I couldn't trust.

On the day of the wedding all of us girls got ready together in the master bedroom, which was the size of my entire home. My little niece Emily was a toddler and was having a ball playing and hiding under the tulle of the skirt of my dress. My eldest niece, Maddison, was quietly lying on my bed, ignoring the mayhem around her, studiously working on the speech I had asked her to give at the reception. I was feeling terribly sick, but managing to hang in there. Bec continued to top me up with cold-and-flu tablets as needed until, suddenly, it was time.

The ceremony was in the garden of the chateau. The wedding party first assembled in the grand entrance hall to walk out to the celebrant. The music I had chosen was k.d. lang's version of

Leonard Cohen's *Hallelujah*, which is still one of my favourite songs. My nieces Maddison and little Emily went first, Emily tottering unsteadily in her tiny flower girl dress. Mum and Nicki followed and then my friend George grabbed my arm, gave me a big kiss and off we went. Almost as soon as I stepped off the cobblestones I regretted my decision not to hire the red carpet that I had thought was over the top, as my cream satin heels sank into the grass and I became stuck. I started to laugh at how ridiculous I must have looked. Poor George had to try and pull me up after every step while I struggled to remain upright. I was almost hysterical with laughter, fear and 'le French flu'. I locked eyes with my sister Hanna who started to cry. For some reason that just sent me into fits of giggles. Perhaps I was high on cold-and-flu medication because I can't explain why I felt like I had been taken over by a kind of drunken hilarity: it was only when I looked up and noticed Brett crying with happiness that the significance of the occasion set in and I allowed myself to feel hopeful. I clung onto that feeling for the rest of the day and for many days to come.

Although the circumstances surrounding my wedding were far from ideal, there was one very good reason why I would never take back that week in France. It was the time spent with my best mate Nicki. She had been sick and was battling chronic pain. The doctors had diagnosed arthritis, although this didn't seem to account for everything that was going on. Nicki has always been one of the most treasured people in my life. She is a tiny thing who moves like a hummingbird, with a wild mane of glossy, curly brown hair and an even wilder laugh. We had bonded over similar childhoods and our way of always looking towards the future rather than dwelling on the past. We understood each other, and we were each other's true north. Seeing her sick petrified me. I didn't know it at the time but my wedding in France was the last time Nicki was able to travel that kind of distance. She went on to be diagnosed with osteo- and rheumatoid arthritis, which was progressing scarily fast and she was later told she had the auto-immune disease Sjögren's syndrome and lupus. She was my matron of honour that day, wearing shoes with the tiniest kitten heel you can imagine. It wasn't until we were home in Australia that I found out that wearing those tiny shoes had put so much pressure on her feet that she had fractured the small bones near her toes. She didn't tell me at the time because she didn't want to worry me. Just another example of her selfless and determined character.

CHAPTER 29

Brett and I came home from our glorious charade and relived a second cocktail-party ceremony for everyone who couldn't make it to France. I can't say why we went through with this, except that I felt obligated to do it all again: I didn't want to let everyone down. Especially Dad and my grandparents who couldn't be there the first time. Again, people had booked flights and hotels, organised sitters and spent time arranging their plans months in advance. Brett went back up to Hamilton Island to complete a shift and didn't get home until a few days before the party.

We both tried to get past what had happened. It was done and irreversible, so we tried to plough forward. As in France, I came down with a terrible flu a few days before the party. On the evening of the party it was cold, but I was so feverish I didn't feel it at all. The wedding party had a Balinese theme,

Eveningwear shoot for my great friend Martin Sanders, produced by the gorgeous Kaz Kingdon. I was in my twenties so the fashion was a little old for me, but they always did fresh young hair and make-up.

with lots of twinkling candles and a fabulous band that had everyone dancing all night. We chose the Manly Life Saving Club as the venue because my family has so much history there. My great-grandfather was the first president and founding member and Dad has served as president for many years.

Despite feeling unwell, I had made the decision to stay strong and try to make the best of the night. At one point I looked up and my oldest and dearest friend, AJ, strolled through the door. He had flown up from Melbourne to surprise me. We snuck off to have a private catch up for a few minutes and as he started asking me questions about the wedding in France and telling me how happy he was for me, I felt my façade slip. I've never been able to hide the truth from AJ and I started to cry. I can't recall his exact words when I told him everything that had happened between Brett and me, but I do remember that he gave me a huge hug and a kiss. We held hands tightly as we walked back down the path to the party inside. I put my game face back on, locked up my sadness and danced all night.

In the aftermath of our weddings, Brett drank a lot and I ran and rode my bike a lot. I hadn't stopped loving him because of what he had done, but I was struggling to find a new normal for us. I watched Brett more closely than I had in the past and it wasn't long before I could see where all our money had gone: booze and gambling. The physical exertion of riding my bike was good therapy for me. I had been training for amateur triathlons for a while and it always gave me such a boost when I completed a difficult ride. I know that in terms of size I was the biggest in the group of riders I trained with, but I was easily as fit as the others. I loved seeing the combination of shock and awe etched on fellow-riders' faces when they saw it was me bearing down on them during a ride. I knew people made a snap judgement about my fitness capabilities when they looked at me, so it was incredibly satisfying to defy their expectations.

As well as the regular exercise I was doing, my work kept me moving. It propelled me forward. I believed in what I was doing and could block everything else out while I was working. As an agent or manager, you become very close to your talent. You find out everything about them: you know intimate details such as their menstrual cycles, as well as their insecurities and their hopes and dreams. They place all their trust in you. It's a huge responsibility and I wasn't about to let the issues in my personal life interfere with my models' trust. I wasn't one to drop the ball. It sounds stressful, but this way of working suited me. I was focused and in control. When I was sitting behind my desk on my phone I felt like I was in charge of my world. It was just in my love life that I felt small and lost and the worst was yet to come.

The more successful I became in my business the more resentful Brett became. I had signed for a credit card for him to use with access to my account and he began to spend money on ridiculous and unnecessary things: long lunches and lots of alcohol, for example. And then there was hundreds of dollars he accrued in parking fines because he either couldn't be bothered finding a legal parking spot or couldn't be bothered moving his car. Eventually, it became too much, so I cut him off. When Brett's job on Hamilton Island ended, our account hovered around empty.

I began to feel desperate about our relationship and where it had landed us. I knew that Brett's parents had a traditional and conservative marriage: the father was the provider and the mother supported every decision. That had been his model of a marriage growing up, but our relationship just couldn't function like that. It wasn't who I was as a person and I obviously couldn't trust Brett's decision-making skills. Why couldn't he see my success as something to be proud of, instead of something he had to hide from or something that undermined him? I was trying to build something for us: I didn't want to see all my hard work go to boys' nights out and nightclubs. I didn't think I was being unreasonable.

Mum and her partner, Terry, gave Brett another chance. Terry had a friend who was the head of a major recruitment company in Sydney. The company was planning to open a trades division and Terry's friend thought that Brett had the personality to go into recruitment. He was charming and funny, he could talk to anyone and he had trade skills, so he could read plans and talk to recruits on a level that a normal agent wasn't able to. He took the job. It didn't pay well but it was a good start.

Although he was working again, Brett's job was not enough to keep us afloat financially. I needed to do something more to stop *BELLA* going under. I decided on real estate. I would scale back and run *BELLA* as I did at the start, checking emails during breaks and working on my marketing at night. Once I got my real estate licence I could build up to a decent wage and with commissions from sales I could afford to employ a staff member for *BELLA* to help with the admin load. So that's exactly what I did. All those years of selling models over the phone worked to my advantage in real estate. Cold-calling was like breathing for me. People can be complicated and emotional, but I dealt with that every day. The marketing plans I could do in my sleep. I flew through my online licence course in a matter of weeks. I even got my auctioneer's licence just in case I needed the extra money on weekends. I got a job quickly with a lovely older couple who were hoping I could help modernise their business. They reminded me of my grandparents and placed a great deal of trust in me. I wanted to do them proud and I agreed to come on and help, but I also knew I had no idea how long I would entertain this partial career change.

I put the word out for someone I could train as a model booker to hold the fort at *BELLA* while I hit the real estate beat. I eventually hired a young woman named Lucy, who had come highly recommended. I needed Lucy to keep it a secret that I was working two jobs, so I needed her to be not only smart and professional, but discreet and discerning. I threw poor Lucy in the deep end and, to her credit, she swam like a fish. We would text each other during the day and I would tell her what to say or what to write in emails. When I went out on sales appointments I would drop in and deal with anything urgent or any documents that required my signature. It was non-stop, and I was shattered at the end of every day.

CHAPTER 30

Our lives went on in this way for a while until one day when I received a call from a good friend to tell me that he had seen Brett in the city with another woman. I hung up the phone as my friend's words continued to ring in my ears: he had said, 'They looked so intimate'. Brett was friendly, I knew that, so maybe he was just with an old friend. Through the noise in my mind a voice rang out loud and clear: 'You have buried yourself in this relationship. You have hidden your soul to make life easier for your husband.' This time I couldn't miss the red flag being waved at me — it was as big as a bus. This was the beginning of the end for us.

I had done so much to try and make our marriage work. I had been forgiving. I had been understanding. I had been caring, encouraging, loving and I had made myself small so that he would have more space — more space to feel like a bigger man.

I was working like a maniac, sometimes 20 hours a day, so that we could afford to pay our bills. I was falling into bed like a zombie every night. Was I doing all this while he was out fucking another woman? Was he with someone else all day before coming home to me, drunk and full of complaints about how hard I was working?

I know most people would have confronted their partner straight away, but I didn't say anything about the phone call at first. I didn't have any actual proof. At this point it was someone else's observation; I hadn't seen anything with my own eyes. It had been such a long time since Brett and I had been in sync, we weren't truly connecting and had pretty much been in crisis mode since the wedding. I think I kept silent at first because I didn't know how to give up on something. It wasn't in my nature and not what I was used to. I needed to know I had tried everything to make my marriage work.

Was it fear that made me stay? Maybe. Fear of failure; fear of giving up on someone I loved; fear of not giving someone a chance to get it together. I'd been in that position. I had needed help and I was lucky that I had it from friends and family. When Brett and I were good, we had so much fun. We had an absolute ball together half the time, it was just enough to keep me trying to have faith and have hope for us. I was also terrified of what he might do to himself if I left. I was scared he would drink himself into the grave. I loved him, but I knew I'd be okay without him. I didn't know if he would be okay without me. I felt responsible for his well-being. I wanted what every person who loves an addict wants: I wanted to save him from himself.

The one thing I hadn't tried in my attempts to save our

David Jones Campaign again. I really loved this shot: it was closer to my usual simple style of clothing, although I hated those shoes!

marriage was to be entirely and unapologetically me. I needed to leave everything on the table. No holding back, no making myself small for Brett's sake. I was going to be 100 per cent me, and if that was something that Brett couldn't handle, then I would have my answer.

The first thing I did was tell Brett that I couldn't keep supporting him financially. I wanted to move my business from home to its own location. If I wasn't supporting Brett I could afford to pay myself a modest wage and even keep Lucy on. I'd need to save some money first, but it was doable. I told Brett that he would need to start paying for half of everything in our household. This included food, rent, bills and even his own beer. It did not go down well. He threw a tantrum that lasted weeks. He was like a teenager who is told they must start paying board to live at home. I tried explaining that it wouldn't matter where he lived, he would still have to contribute to rent and bills and that I needed him to help me out. I didn't think my expectations were unreasonable. It was about time he grew up. He did it in the end, but he always made me feel like I was stealing his money. I just needed him to pay his share, I wasn't asking him to pay all the bills as I had been doing for years.

We struggled on like this for a while before the universe threw me a bone, as it often does when you least expect it. I received a call from one of my old modelling clients and all-round wonderful person, Melanie Schwarz. Melanie worked as head of marketing for the size 12+ clothing label, Taking Shape. She was calling me to let me know that Taking Shape had recently conducted a survey with their top 100 customers to find out which fashion model they had liked the most over the years. Turns out, it was me. I was stunned. I had no idea that was what she would say: I thought she was going to tell me it was one of my models.

I had put modelling to bed years before. It wasn't something I ever thought I would do again. Mel went on to ask me if I would come out of retirement to shoot a big campaign. I probably wouldn't have gone back in front of the camera for anyone else, but it was also coming from my early mentor at Myer, Alla, who had since become the CEO of Taking Shape. I was so grateful for the acknowledgement and to be asked, but I was torn — it's not the done thing for agents to model. It's considered a conflict of interest. In the end though, I decided I had to go for it. I was on the verge of losing everything and this was an opportunity to save my business. I would commit to modelling exclusively for Mel and Alla's label and I was happy for them to do whatever they wanted with my look.

It started as one shoot and ended up being a two-year collaboration. Throughout the project I was given about 15 different hair colours and just as many cuts and styles. It apparently became a 'thing' with the customers. They would watch out for my latest hairstyle in the most recent catalogue and take my shots to their hairdresser to get the same look. It made a huge difference to my life and to the continued existence of *BELLA*. I am eternally grateful to Alla, Melanie and the customers who granted me that opportunity.

It wasn't long after beginning my contract with Taking Shape that I managed to save enough money to be able to resign from the real estate agency. I could afford to rent office space and pay wages for about three months. I was ecstatic, but Brett was furious that I hadn't consulted him about my plans for the business. We got into a huge fight and everything came out. We found ourselves standing in the kitchen, facing off, staring down the last five years of our relationship, when it dawned on me: I couldn't save Brett. I had been forgiving of all his lies and betrayals, all his bad behaviour and poor decisions because I had been hoping that my love would be enough to make him a better person. As the tears streamed down my cheeks I grabbed his face with both hands and said, 'How is it possible to love and hate someone at the same time?' With a jolt, I recalled feeling the exact same way about Dad all those years ago. It was finally over between us and we decided to separate. Brett was going to go and stay with his brother and I was going to stay in the house we were renting with Dad out the back. It made sense. Not least because I was the only one who could afford it.

CHAPTER 31

BELLA was full steam ahead, so I moved into an office space in Manly. Not an easy feat, considering my budget, but I had noticed that the energy around me had shifted after my marriage ended and things were starting to fall into place. I also moved into a house closer to the office; the only rental I could afford that would let me have my little Harry dog. It was more of a shack really. There was no insulation, so it was freezing in winter and roasting in summer. I'm pretty sure the backyard hadn't been tended for 100 years and it took all my willpower to brave the wilds and go out there to use the laundry. Dad was still recovering from his illness, so he moved with me as well. We affectionately referred to our new home as 'the house of mould', because a damp green mould would slowly creep up the walls from the dingy storage area under the house if you didn't keep all the windows open, all the time. To be honest, everything about the place was bloody depressing. The only thing keeping the bulldozers from the door was my lease. Still, it was the best I could do, so I made the most of it.

My models were busier than ever. We were getting lots of press about body-image issues and reaching a much wider audience than ever before. I was signing models to top agencies all over the world and they were going on to do incredibly well: some were even considered top models internationally.

The way agencies function is that they set up working relationships with 'sister' agencies around the world. In Australia, because our market is comparably small, we scout and develop the models and, when they get to the right stage in their careers, we look for bigger markets where the models can make more money and have better opportunities. Every agency has a different network of contacts internationally. Essentially there's something of an international network which allows us to share models. The founding agency or agent, that the model chooses to be their primary manager, places models with this worldwide network and manages the model's diary and obligations from the 'mother' office, as we call it. This is how and why models travel so much and why agents can never rely on getting a full night's sleep.

Around the time I moved the business into the Manly office, I was introduced to a young woman called Robyn Lawley. Robyn had been put on to *BELLA* after an art director associate noticed her at a casting. The director called me to say that she had just seen a stunning young model who was outside the rigid requirements of the mainstream fashion market, but who was too beautiful to ignore. Apparently, Robyn had also seen one of my models featured in a magazine editorial, so she was also keen to get in touch with me. We arranged to meet.

The second I opened the door I was floored; she was just incredible. She wasn't wearing any make-up and I could see that her bone structure was amazing. I could instantly envision the kind of career she could have. We chatted for ages about her experiences with fashion and modelling and how difficult it had been for her to maintain a size 8–10. We talked about her personal life and her travels overseas. I was beginning to see that not only was she incredibly beautiful, she was also super-smart and mature. I signed her straight away and told her I wanted her to be completely herself: I wanted her to know that I wouldn't be asking her to lose weight or change anything about her appearance. I wanted her to be her natural, healthy weight. She told me later that she almost didn't believe what I was saying. She had been to so many castings and potential signings that started out positively, but always ended with a caveat around needing to lose weight.

As soon as Robyn left, I rang Mum and said: 'I've just signed the world's next supermodel.'

Polaroid from a test shoot with Jon Waddy in his studio in Redfern when I was about 26 years old. Jon is Dad's best friend and an amazing photographer: he shot most of Mum's fashion covers over the years. He is also the person responsible for introducing my parents.

CHAPTER 32

Proclaiming Robyn to be the next international supermodel was a bold prediction but, as it turned out, I was right. Robyn's career skyrocketed. Since signing with *BELLA* Robyn has gone on to do all the things I hoped for her and more. She has been the trailblazer I knew she could be and I'm so incredibly proud of her. Not least because through it all she has remained humble, grateful and a passionate advocate for body acceptance on a global scale.

Robyn has an extensive CV of groundbreaking achievements in the world of fashion and beauty, including appearing in *Vogue Italia* and a guest appearance on the *Ellen* show that has been viewed over a million times. These are just a couple of her stand-out triumphs; there are dozens of high-profile magazine covers also — too many to mention. However, my particular favourite is one that also brought me intense personal and professional satisfaction. I'm talking about the time she booked an eight-page high fashion spread in Australian *Vogue*.

Vogue Australia is the pinnacle of all things high fashion in this country. But it's not just on our home shores that the publication is so highly regarded. *Vogue Australia* has a reputation internationally for pushing boundaries and creating exclusive and innovative editorial looks. To be featured in its pages is a fashion coup for designers, photographers, stylists and models. Getting a model of mine to feature in *Vogue* had been something of a holy grail for me from the moment *BELLA* came into existence. So, when the inimitable editor of Australian *Vogue*, Kirstie Clements, called to book Robyn for an editorial shoot, I was beside myself with excitement and pride. And the news just got better and better. Kirstie also wanted to let us know that she would be introducing Robyn and talking about the importance of her influence on fashion and beauty in her editor's letter. This is what she had to say about Robyn in her *Vogue Australia* column of September 2011:

> *This is the first time* Vogue Australia *has shot a larger model and, of course, now that we have done it, I ask myself why we didn't do it sooner. But that's because Robyn is especially gorgeous. I went to the shoot to meet her and was transfixed by her beauty and poise. She is a truly super-duper model. When a plus-size model first turns up to the studio, she may be an anomaly to a team normally used to working with size 6's, but once photographer Max Doyle started shooting Robyn, we quickly readjusted our preconceived notions of beauty. 'She doesn't actually look plus size to me at all now,' I told a colleague on set.*

I burst into tears when I read what Kirstie had written. It had taken me thousands of hours over so many years to finally make a crack in what had increasingly seemed like the impenetrable wall around Australian *Vogue*. And Kirstie didn't stop there. *Vogue* asked if I would provide a brief interview for Robyn's issue. I couldn't say yes fast enough and as soon as they sent through the questions I answered as quickly as I could with everything they'd asked for, and more. The features editor, Alexandra Spring, rang me a short time later to tell me that they thought what I had written deserved to be a full article and that they were going to publish it as such. I was over the moon. In that same issue that featured an eight-page spread of my gorgeous Robyn, they also published a two-page story on the importance of curve models called 'Why Plus Matters', written by me. It was an incredible double win for diversity.

...

Robyn is just one of so many positive and inspiring stories I've witnessed over the years. The greatest satisfaction I gain from my work is watching the change in the young women I sign once they start working as models. Often, they come in for their first meeting nervous and insecure because they have been told throughout their teenage or young adult life that they are too fat to be considered attractive. They have disengaged from their bodies. Once they start working and find acceptance and support and they start to understand that they're being booked as a model not despite their size but because they are beautiful, we start to see this incredible change. The way they carry themselves shifts and you can feel the happiness radiate from them. They stand taller; become more adventurous with their fashion choices and they become more engaged in life.

I've had dozens and dozens of thank-you letters and emails from the families of my models; grateful that we have helped bring happiness to their daughter, sister, niece or cousin's life, and I feel the same. I believe that self-acceptance is the most powerful and joyful feeling there is, so to see it played out in my business every day is enormously satisfying and gratifying. To see it played out in the pages of Australia's premier fashion magazine was the icing on the cake. I want every woman to feel self-acceptance and I know that my models help put women on that path. This is what drives me to get up every day and keep pushing the boundaries.

CHAPTER 33

Throughout my career I have experienced breathtaking highs like Robyn's feature in Australian *Vogue*, but I have also had to deal with some career lows.

There's the seemingly endless number of small challenges, like shaving a model's legs before a runway walk; racing off set to buy tampons; babysitting models' children and looking after a model's dog. The daily requests can be literally anything. I've also had clashes with clients, usually with people who take themselves too seriously or enjoy making life difficult for absolutely no good reason other than a power trip. I won't tolerate my models being treated badly, so there has been the odd clash with a client who I believe has treated my models unfairly or without the respect they deserve.

There was one particular lowlight that perfectly illustrates the negativity and discrimination that my models faced on a

Embracing your body with positive vibes leads to more openness, conscientiousness and extroversion.

'How you feel about your body has a "huge" affect on how happy you are', Macaela Mackenzie, published online at shape.com, 12 May 2016

This was one of my favourite campaign shoots for David Jones. They had booked me for two seasons and wanted to book me again, but were worried about the shots starting to look too similar. So I dyed my hair red! I appeared in many shoots that winter – Westfield, Berlei, Cosmopolitan – as a redhead.

regular basis. It just so happens that this incident played out at a high-profile national event: Sydney Fashion Week.

As part of Fashion Week, one of the country's most successful ready-to-wear retailers wanted to do an exclusive plus-size runway. This decision on its own wasn't really a problem for me. Of course, I would have much preferred that they didn't segregate the models this way and I would have liked to have seen curve and plus-size models alongside 'straight' models on all the runways throughout the week (as we had for Peter Morrissey, Camilla and Bonds). But I went along with the plus-size runway idea because it was too big an event to stay away from.

The problem for me arose when I found out that the retailer wanted to include 'street cast' women in the show alongside my models. I disagreed with this decision passionately. What the retailer wanted was women with absolutely no runway or modelling experience walking alongside my professionally trained models. I pleaded with them not to do it. There was no other runway in Fashion Week that was using people with no experience. I felt like they were trying to say that my models were somehow less professional than the 'straight' models. Were they making a mockery of the profession because of a size difference? I contacted every person involved in the event to argue my point and have the decision reversed.

The reason I was so incensed was because the catwalk is an artform. There is a very particular way a runway model walks to show the clothes off to their full advantage. Learning that skill can take months of preparation and training for those who don't have a natural gait or grace. Professional models make it look easy: that's part of their skill. I knew that 'street cast' women would not have the same skills and their lack of professionalism (through no fault of their own, I must add) would undermine the work of my models. Unfortunately, my protests at Sydney Fashion Week fell on deaf ears and the producers of the show ignored my argument. I was forced to make a difficult call: I didn't want my models to miss out on an opportunity to walk in one of the country's premier fashion events, so we decided to go ahead. The show made headlines around the country for all the wrong reasons. The press had a field day pointing out that the models stomped and hurled themselves down the runway in a chaotic procession. My models stood out like shining stars, bless their hearts. They tried their best to cover for the untrained women who forgot when to turn, where to turn, or even how to turn, but it wasn't enough. The show was a farce and I was furious. What could have been a game-changing moment — proving the place for diverse sizes on the runway — turned into validation for all the designers who had never wanted to book a plus-size model for their shows. It took years to recover from that event in terms of show bookings and I'm still filthy that no-one listened to me.

There are many examples of the kind of prejudice we experienced at Fashion Week. We have had to work twice as hard as every other agency to make our mark. I've had to continually hound and harass magazine editors to book my models for the simplest shoots. The mainstream fashion world has traditionally been unable to see plus-size models as fashionable; the idea has been totally at odds with its way of existing. I knew that, so I have always been prepared to be persistent. That's not to say that I don't find it frustrating. Of course, I get sick of repeatedly explaining what I see as obvious, but repetition is the way we learn and educating people is the way we change the world. Patience is an underdeveloped skill in our world of immediate gratification.

While I've needed endless patience and the persuasive skills of a lawyer to have the message heard, I have also had to adjust to the speed with which the plus-size model industry has grown. This has caused us some teething problems. We went from banging down doors to trying to keep up with the wave of change. What had previously been known almost exclusively as the plus-size industry was being rebranded as 'curve'. I couldn't be happier with the change in terminology: I had been uncomfortable referring to women as plus-size for a long time now. The only problem I had with the advent of 'curve' was that it became the hot topic all over the fashion world. More and more models bigger than size 10 were being signed to big agencies, getting big contracts and securing amazing magazine editorial opportunities — we could barely keep up. It was fast becoming big business, with a lot of money to be earned and everyone wanted the same thing at the same time.

Of course, that's not how it works, so I have had to balance expectations with the complicated network of decision-makers who book models for different reasons based on different trends. When new models were 'discovered' by clients and booked for shoots over the models who believed they had 'earned their stripes', I often ended up as piggy in the middle. I've had to try and remain neutral and ride it out. I have been carrying out a delicate juggling act for many years now.

Dealing with so many different models and their vastly different personalities also poses a continual set of challenges each day. And, boy, have we had some doozies! I've had a young model who shoplifted from a store in which she featured on all the campaign posters, including the ones inside the store! I've had a model who was so sensationally needy and addicted to drama that every time I was out of the office for a personal day she would experience a crisis that only I could solve. Boyfriends caused constant issues: navigating all the travel and attention is stressful for relationships and I've had many models choose their relationship over a career. I have also had a model, who I put years of work and my own money into developing, sign with another agency as soon as the big money started rolling in. These circumstances aside, I haven't had many models leave my agency and that's something that makes me proud. I keep an open door (unless someone has been especially vile) because I believe that everyone is allowed lapses in judgement. God knows, I've had a few! In this industry, having an agent who really cares for you and makes sure to care for your garden so you can grow is the most crucial relationship a model or artist can foster.

CHAPTER 34

In the year leading up to what I now call 'the crash', I began to feel overwhelmed. For a long time I had been having trouble managing the symptoms of what had been diagnosed as PTSD, depression and bipolar disorder. To get on top of the debilitating fatigue, insomnia and depression I was integrating natural therapies with a low-dose selective serotonin reuptake inhibitor (SSRI). However, I had also started experiencing intense sensory flashbacks — as many as 15 on the worst days. During a flashback my body would seize up; there was no spasming or shaking, I would just freeze for up to 20 seconds. From the outside I was told that I looked still and vacant. If I tried to speak it apparently sounded like nonsense. Inside my mind it felt like I was encased in my childhood. It felt quite literally that I was back there. I could smell everything, taste everything, hear everything and then, bam! I'd find myself back sitting on my couch at home or at my desk at work or wherever I happened to be when it came on. Once it happened when I was driving Nicki down the coast for a weekend away. It scared the hell out of her because she could see that I was not 'there', even though I was still functioning enough to drive.

I didn't feel that the diagnoses I'd been given for depression, PTSD and bipolar could account for the seizures I was experiencing, so I sought out all manner of medical opinions. I was admitted to hospital several times, but the results of the tests showed nothing. I went to see specialists for brain scans to determine if it was epilepsy, but the results were negative. The neurosurgeon was stumped. In the end all he could come up with was a theory that extreme stress was causing my brain to glitch, like an overloaded computer.

To tackle the symptoms on my own, I became a total health freak. I did everything right: no drinking; clean eating; every vitamin ever made was in my fridge; I was exercising like a crazy person to try to wear myself out enough to sleep through the night. After about six months of living like this, the seizures stopped. For a brief while I felt like it had been a bump in the road. But then came the fatigue. I couldn't seem to get enough sleep. I'd wake up from eight hours sleep and want to go straight back to bed. When I was up and moving it was like trying to wade through thick mud. Luckily, I was running my business from my home office at the time, so I could work all day in my pyjamas. I would suffer like this for a week and then the following week I would feel fine. I could go for months with no symptoms and then the heaviness would come back. No-one could figure out what was going on, so it was put down to

Harry dog's first Christmas at my Nana's house, 1999.

stress, depression and PTSD. The thing was, though, I didn't feel depressed, just bloody frustrated.

On top of the heaviness I began to experience a creeping pain in my neck and shoulders that would travel down my arms and back and then into my legs. It didn't matter how many stretches I did to try and loosen my muscles, they always felt so tight that they could snap. Again, I put it down to my work: spending all that time on a computer and phone. I had read a lot about how emotional stress and pain could manifest physically, so it seemed feasible. Even though it appeared that I had a rational explanation for what was happening, I struggled to cope with the pain and discomfort. This is when I turned to alcohol in a big way. In my wilder, younger days I had never been a daily drinker, it was just letting loose on the weekends. When Brett and I were married we would drink together most nights, but now I noticed that when I drank it relieved the pain. The alcohol would make me feel almost immediately better. So it became a crutch. I knew that if I was feeling like crap I could just have a few drinks and the pain would go away. It wasn't long before a few drinks became a bottle or two.

I resigned myself to thinking that I was a bipolar depressive person who drank a little too much and that was to be my lot in life. I asked around my girlfriends if they thought I was drinking too much and most said they thought it was about normal. Okay, I thought, I'm just a girl who likes a drink. Deep down though, I knew that I was starting to depend on the alcohol and with Dad's history I was scared. I would go for long periods without alcohol just to check I wasn't addicted, though fearfully I wondered if I could keep control of it over the long haul.

The year of 'the crash' I started experiencing chest pains and heart palpitations. They would be so uncomfortable that I would wake up in the middle of the night. As well as the pain in my chest, my whole body felt like it was on fire and my hands and feet had pins and needles. I was eating healthily and exercising all the time (triathlon training, no less); I was taking vitamins and doing all my stretching; but I was still drinking every night. One bottle had become two because it was the only thing that gave me any relief. I was also running the business, travelling the world and achieving all the goals I had set for myself when I started *BELLA*. I wanted to keep pushing through because I believed in what I was doing. I kept telling myself that what I was working towards was something much bigger than myself and my personal health. So I kept going.

Then one evening everything stopped. Fourteen hours of my life disappeared, and I woke up surrounded by my loved ones. I was in a total daze. I couldn't figure out what was going on. Why was everyone standing around me with concerned looks on their faces? It was a Sunday morning, I sat stunned, listening to the accounts of what I'd said and done.

They told me I had tried to call my sisters and Mum very late at night and when no-one answered I put a post on Facebook asking for someone to send the police to my home because I'd been raped. The police came, followed by my girlfriend Brenda who found me curled up in the foetal position on my bed, mumbling incoherently. All the doors and windows were open in the house, so they went hunting for my phone to call my family. Two of my best friends, Karen and Jon, arrived and Karen got into bed with me. She remembers me talking in a small child's voice and when Dad turned up and came into the room I began screaming at him to get out, over and over. Karen says I told her about the man who raped me. I was familiar with the theme. I knew that the man she was telling me about was the family friend who had made me so uncomfortable when I was a child. The police couldn't find any evidence of someone having been in my home or any evidence that I had been attacked, so my friends and family went through my kitchen and bins looking for any signs of drugs that I might have taken. There was nothing but a couple of bottles of wine. I have absolutely no recollection of doing or saying any of it. The medical term for what I experienced is a psychotic break.

My sister Skye arrived and took me to a doctor the next day to try and figure out how I had got into such a terrifying state. Although my doctor had been warning me to slow down for years, I hadn't wanted to listen. They were now telling me that they had no other answers for me but to take it easy and seek counselling. My tightly sealed internal containers had started to leak and there was no more storage space left for the emotional baggage I was carrying. I was shaky, tired and humiliated, but didn't know how to sit at home and do nothing. I didn't want to be alone worrying about my sanity, so I took one day off after 'the crash' and went back to work.

CHAPTER 35

During the year of 'the crash' I was approached by the ABC to appear in an episode of their award-winning documentary series *Australian Story*. The producers thought that the combination of my fight for body image diversity and my family history would make for compelling viewing. I saw it as an opportunity to look forward and to share my experiences so that anyone else who had experienced something similar wouldn't feel so alone. I was honoured to be asked, but Dad was very uncomfortable with the prospect. Although Dad had found some peace in terms of his past as an alcoholic, he was very nervous about giving up control over how the story was told. I understood his fear: he was still unable to remember huge chunks of his life and my sisters, Mum and I had never spoken about those dark days publicly before. He panicked and began to dump an enormous amount of mouldy old baggage on me. I tried to explain to him that the ABC wanted *my* story and the truth about *my* life. He didn't have the right to tell me that my story couldn't be told, and I needed him to know that I believed that I could help others who had lived through similar scenarios if I opened up. I promised him that I wouldn't go into too much detail and I made the producers promise they wouldn't dig too deeply into that part of my life. I kept my word and so did the producers of the show, but throughout the six months of filming he made himself such a burden that I was emotionally and physically exhausted when we finally wrapped.

When I look back now on how my *Australian Story* was put together, I think that it was handled elegantly and honourably, and many people have written to me to thank me for opening up about that part of our lives, as it has helped them in a profound way. At the time though, the process stripped away virtually all my defences and left me facing the future with very little in the tank. I vowed to make myself a priority.

I headed into the new year with the best of intentions. I wasn't going to work late into the night as I had done for years. I would make sure that I had a minimum of six hours sleep every night. I set a new timetable for work and would only take calls and answer emails between 5am and 9pm. I would take up a hobby, just for fun. I was going to take an hour in the afternoon every day to walk along the waterfront with my Harry dog. I was going to decompress and breathe in the salty air. I bought myself a vintage boat that I was going to restore and get out on the water, my happiest place. I had wanted a boat for years, but had been waiting for someone to buy one with. Now I thought, 'What the hell am I waiting for?

I may never meet someone who likes boats.' So, I bought one myself and started the year sanding and painting; bobbing around on the water with a fresh perspective on personal health.

As it turned out, however, the universe wasn't done testing me quite yet. In the space of two months I was rocked by the death of both my darling little Harry dog and my steadfast and wonderful Nana. It was a devastating double blow. From a very young age, Nana and I had been close. She was a tough cookie and didn't suffer fools, but I was never put off by her sharp tongue; I saw through that to her golden heart. She would say things to me like, 'You'll be the death of me,' and I'd fire back with, 'Angry old people last the longest'. She would look at me like murder, but then laugh her head off. That was us. Some of my happiest childhood memories are of my cousins and me making up and performing plays and musical pieces for everyone at Nana and Grandpa's house. We were safe and silly and didn't have any worries with Nana watching over us.

I loved that woman so much. I understood her fear and her pain, her distrust and her fierce, no-nonsense love. It was unconditional and brutally honest and, in my life, that honesty was a tonic. 'Look at yourself,' she would say. 'It starts with you... if you don't like something, change it.' Or, 'If you don't know what to do, do nothing'. I didn't understand that one until later in life, but it became one of my rules for living. It just means don't react to everything that's going on around you without thinking. Take your time to find a solution. Don't be a hothead, make a plan.

Without the rock-solid presence of my Nana and the constant joy from my little Harry, I was shaken to the core. Over the

With my sisters and niece at my wedding to Brett in France. Despite all the drama of the week and 'le French flu', we made the best of it. I was pretty high on French cold and flu tablets by this stage in the day!

next few months I was in so much physical and emotional pain it felt like I was watching a storm coming through the heads of Sydney Harbour. Big black clouds, heavy with rain. I felt frozen in place watching it coming at me, not knowing how long I had before I felt its force. I was almost mesmerised by the intensity of it. I thought, 'This time it's too big, I can't escape.' I rang Mum: 'I need help,' I said. 'It's coming for me and I don't think I have the strength to survive it.'

For the first time ever, I couldn't get myself up. I had always been able to find the strength before to haul myself to my feet, to get up and fight, but now I was totally empty and truly afraid for my life. Within a day Mum had researched all over the world to find somewhere I could go to recover in a safe place. She settled on a rehabilitation facility in Thailand.

I dragged myself onto that plane feeling defeated and so, so sad. I was done in and knew that if I didn't do something drastic, I wouldn't make it through this time. I felt the weight of responsibility on my shoulders too; there were so many people who relied on me and who needed me to keep going. If I couldn't do it for me, then I had to for all the people who needed to see me get up and keep going. This feeling was enough to get me halfway around the world to the facility that Mum told me specialised in cognitive behaviour therapy (CBT).

CHAPTER 36

I was scared, not in the least because I was worried that I might come out the other end so changed or confused from looking back into my life that I might never be 'me' again. I didn't want to turn into a whining nut job whom no-one wanted around. I didn't want to become one of those people who talked about themselves incessantly under the guise of spiritual enlightenment. I've met people like that; people who floated through their life, lost, unable to reconcile themselves or their thoughts because they pushed too far and didn't have a guide to walk them back to the path. I didn't want that, but I had run out of options.

I landed in Bangkok and was met by a car that would take me on a six-hour drive south to the facility. The last drink I'd had was about three weeks earlier, at my Nana's funeral, but the staff at the facility was adamant that I provide a blood and urine sample. I tried to explain that I wasn't there for substance-abuse rehab: I was a workaholic who wanted to learn CBT so I could balance myself out. I thought that it would help me manage all the stress and give me new tools to rely on rather than work and wine. I was hoping that I could dig up whatever issues I had buried deep in my soul and get them out in a safe environment so that I never had to experience another year like the one I'd just had. It was clear to me that my own methods of self-medication and self-help had not been effective over the long term. I thought that this trip was going to be like a health retreat with psychological counselling. But it turns out this wasn't exactly what my family had planned. They had told the facility that they were concerned about my drinking and they thought that I was a high-functioning alcoholic. They may have been right, so I let them do all the tests and waited in the sweltering heat outside my room while they checked the results.

My room was inside a flat squat building, covered in white stucco with blue trim. I guessed it was an attempt to make it look Mediterranean, but the effect it achieved was far from European chic and more of dirty mental hospital from a horror movie. There was nothing here that was like the website Mum had sent me. 'What the fuck have I got myself into?' I thought.

The next morning, I woke early and went outside. I could see some other early risers walking towards a shed-like building about 100 metres away. I decided to follow. When I filed in with everyone else I could see that it was where breakfast was served. I sat down beside a beautiful woman who introduced herself as Christine. She explained that we were currently in a holding area where they assessed the severity of your problem. If you needed drying out, you would stay in the hospital facility and if you didn't then they sent you on to the 'retreat' facility. Thank goodness!

Drug addicts and alcoholics consistently lie about their level of addiction, so the retreat used the medical centre as a kind of assessment zone. They needed to detox the guests safely so that no-one died coming off hard drugs or booze. I met a guy in there who had been in hospital on a drip for a week while they tried to detox him safely, that's how full of substances he was.

I was cleared and swiftly sent another few hours south to the retreat. It couldn't have been more different from the holding facility. This place was everything I had been hoping for. It was like a five-star hotel, with the only difference being that there was a timetable of classes all day. We were an eclectic bunch of guests. I met lawyers, bankers, CEOs, doctors, strippers, court reporters and school principals, just to name a few. They were successful people from all walks of life, all here to wrestle with whichever coping mechanism had overtaken their lives. Our days were carefully orchestrated and almost every hour accounted for from sunrise to sunset. We started at 7am with either swimming or yoga then breakfast, followed by various classes from group therapy sessions to one-on-one meetings and personal training, all based on the CBT curriculum. I threw myself into it with everything I had. The treatments forced me to face some hard truths about my life, who I am and why I was like that.

My excellent resident psychologist, Ray, helped me to understand that my biggest issue was a sense of unworthiness. I was unable to give myself a break or to feel like I was deserving of success. The only way I could feel like I deserved any of my success was if I was running myself into the ground to do it. It became clear to me over the next month that throughout my whole life I had been told I wasn't worthy. That I was fat, therefore lazy and stupid. This judgement came from everywhere: from the people closest to me, from people on the street and from society as a whole. I began to understand my obsession with work. What I was doing was about justifying my right to exist.

I came to realise that, as much as I wanted to change the world's attitude to women and beauty, and as hard as I was working for it every day, I still had not accepted that I deserved to be thought of that way. I needed to believe in myself that I was beautiful and worthy of love and respect. I had wanted to believe, but in the deepest part of my soul, I didn't pass my own judgement. I had been brainwashed too. Learning all of this shocked the hell out of me. Of all the things I thought were holding me back, it had never occurred to me that my own soul didn't truly accept the words that came out of my mouth. I had been playing at accepting myself; putting on a show. All those times I acted like I was so sure of myself: skinny-dipping naked in front of 20 people; walking down streets naked on a dare; wearing a bikini to the beach — it was all an act of defiance. I was playing the role of rebel, not letting other people put limitations on me. It was a 'fuck you' to the world, not an expression of true acceptance.

I felt a weight lift off my soul. Digging so deep for this truth and knowing the pain I had experienced was like nothing I had ever felt before. The revelation took over my body and I began to purge myself of the self-hate. I got sick, very sick. I threw up for four days. I was feverish and hallucinating: I was talking to my dead grandparents and my Harry dog, pleading for help from them, sobbing uncontrollably. It felt like a lifetime of humiliation, anger and fear was being expelled from my body. On the fourth day I was able to get up. I walked to dinner and sat next to Christine and told her what had happened. She hugged me — a great big bear hug so full of love — and she said, 'You are transformed'. And she was right: that is exactly how I felt and how I feel today.

Mum and Grandpa at my wedding in Manly. Grandpa had Parkinson's and this was the last time he was able to travel interstate. He was such a beautiful human being; Mum is very like him in character.

CHAPTER 37

When I came home from Thailand I took some time to digest all I had learned there. I felt a lot lighter. My head was clearer and my inner voice was getting stronger as I worked to rewire my way of thinking about myself. I learned to identify which thoughts were mine and which came from external forces that, despite the fact that I was morally opposed to them, I had internalised. I dug in and ripped out all those old stubborn root systems and started replanting my garden with the fruits and flowers I chose for myself.

I decided while I was in Thailand that it was time to move out of my house and start afresh. There were too many memories stashed in that house. I kept expecting to see my Harry dog every time I opened the front door or got into bed at night. I had felt the worst bouts of illness there and my eventual collapse had happened in the lounge room.

I have never lived without a dog. Not having one was like missing a limb. So I decided to start the search for my new life partner. One night while looking at Facebook I found a dog rescue page and landed on a photo of a bedraggled little thing that had recently been saved from a kill shelter. I swear I could hear Harry give his blessing to this sad-looking dog — I could feel him telling me, 'She's the one, she needs you'. Two days later Billy was mine. I went to pick her up from her foster mum, Kerrin, who told me that Billy had been badly neglected. She had had no socialisation or training, but she was a sweetheart. I could see in her eyes she was easily overwhelmed by attention, but that she loved being cuddled. So off we went together from the western suburbs to the northern beaches of Sydney.

Billy was frightened of everything at first. She had never even been walked outside on the street because she had spent her whole life up to this point in a small courtyard. Bikes, cars, people, other dogs, even grass were all new to her. The first time I took her to the beach she sat as still as a statue, amazed by the water, before she slowly turned to look at me, like a child seeing the ocean for the first time.

With Billy by my side, I was ready to find my new home. I bought a lovely old house on Sydney Harbour with views through the famous Heads. There's an off-lead dog park running along the water and a string of picturesque coves for swimming that start at the end of the street where I now moor my boat. I had promised Harry that I would get him there one day, because it was our favourite place to be. I have him with me, in a little urn facing the water and I give him a kiss whenever I walk by.

When I bought the house it was a crumbling 120-year-old mess that hadn't been touched for 65 years. The bones were beautiful but the whole place was covered in dust and dirt. There was evidence that possums, birds and rats had made their home there for the best part of a century. The night before I moved in I began to have second thoughts. It was an epic feat just to get her clean. I had professional cleaners in twice to try and cut through the decades of grease and black mould. God knows what the dusty old cellar had once been used for — I ended up covering the whole thing in floorboards to make it less creepy.

Over the months of painting, sanding, replacing floorboards and ripping out old cabinets I could feel the presence of the previous owner, Beth, who had lived there for 65 years. I felt like she approved and was happy to see someone love her home as much as she did. I enjoyed focusing on bringing out the beauty in something that had been so neglected.

I had bought the worst house on the best street and my real estate experience told me that I'd done the right thing. She was a lot of work, but she is my dream home and my safe place in the world. She responded well to a bit of love, as most things do. The day I picked up the keys Mum and I stood on the front verandah looking out at Sydney Harbour and burst into tears. We didn't need to say a word, we silently acknowledged everything I had been through to get to that point.

A few months before moving into my new home I had a breakthrough with my chronic illnesses and near constant pain. I had finally found a diagnosis. It is a condition known as fibromyalgia. Every person who suffers from 'fibro' experiences it slightly differently, but common to most is widespread pain and tenderness through the body, extreme fatigue and problems with memory and concentration. It's also known to bring on the symptoms of depression when the patient is experiencing a flare up. It's a misunderstood disorder that millions of people worldwide struggle with every day and there is very little research or funding for a cure. In Australia, fibro affects two to five per cent of the population and that number is mostly women aged between 20 and 50.

Although it was an enormous relief to finally be able to put a name to what I had been suffering, I don't like to talk about it much and in fact many of my models and friends who know I have it have forgotten and only remember if I mention I have a treatment or if I'm experiencing a flare up. There is no cure, but the symptoms can be managed. I try not to think much about what I can't do because of fibro and concentrate on everything I can do.

Getting the diagnosis has also helped me to understand why drinking alcohol was one of the only ways I could be pain free. Because alcohol is a central nervous system anaesthetic, it helped to numb the pain receptors in my brain. There has been medical research done, including one study which found that 'low to moderate alcohol consumption may lower fibromyalgia symptoms and improve quality of life' ('Association between alcohol consumption and symptom severity and quality of life in patients with fibromyalgia', Chul H Kim et al, *Arthritis Research & Therapy*, 2013). For me, now, it's a combination of factors which help to manage my fibro symptoms. I am careful to not push myself too hard when I begin to experience the onset of a flare up. I know that I need to rest and avoid stress as much as possible. I've come to terms with my condition and aim to just live my life to the best of my abilities.

Moving into my beautiful house on the water was like a new beginning for me and my little Billy. It felt like a chapter of my life had closed and I was ready for what was to come. Billy took to her new life as though she had never experienced the awfulness of her past. She is now the princess of my world. Every day she comes in to work with me, running in the door and through reception before jumping into everyone's open arms for a cuddle and kisses. Her confidence and sass bring me so much happiness every single day.

CHAPTER 38

I was slowly settling into life in my new home next to the water; most of the work had been done to turn it from crumbling wreck to clean and habitable, but there seemed to always be another small job that needed doing, so it wasn't unusual that I was walking the aisles of the local hardware store one day when I received a phone call from an old friend, Dave.

I hadn't seen Dave for years, but we had kept in touch, mainly because we were both close to our mutual friend, Sarah. She was our beautiful, open-hearted, sensitive girl. A few years earlier Sarah's mother had passed away and left a hole in her heart so vast that it seemed no amount of love could fill it up. All her friends, myself and Dave included, had tried our best to help her through her heartbreak, but she had so little resilience. She tried to mask her pain with alcohol, drugs and terrible relationships. There were many times when Dave and I had

Dad and me at my second wedding to Brett in Manly. There's nothing like making the same mistake twice! Seriously though, I'm glad I did it because it meant so much to Dad and my grandparents to be there.

called the police or the ambulance because we feared the worst, and we both agreed that her situation had become even more perilous when she moved interstate with her emotionally abusive partner. I watched as all her sweetness was drained away by this horrible man, who once even admitted to me that he only stayed with Sarah because he had promised her mother when she was dying that he would take care of her. He was superstitious about breaking that promise, so provided a roof over Sarah's head, but very little else.

Sarah's boyfriend was fixated on her appearance and would criticise her ruthlessly about the way she looked. He would also lose his temper if she didn't keep the house in order. Everything had to be perfect. If the house wasn't immaculate he would lose the plot. If his three-course dinner wasn't served on time or to his liking, he would rant and stomp around the house like a madman and call her every name under the sun, frequently reminding her how useless she was. He would yell at her, 'Useless, hopeless, stupid, fat — who would want you?' constantly undermining her already shockingly low self-esteem. His shirts needed to be ironed, washing needed to be done; all the housework taken care of. These were all things that Sarah was expected to do because she was a woman.

He and I hated each other. I thought he was a neanderthal and he hated my independent, free- thinking personality. He was afraid I would influence Sarah to think more for herself and that might ruin the easy life he had going for himself. I openly challenged him to conversation about his archaic way of thinking because I wanted to show her that he wasn't always right. I think he is the only person I've truly despised in my whole life. Even when Sarah was at her sickest and most desperately drug and alcohol dependent, he refused to concede that counselling, rehab, or antidepressants could help her. He refused to acknowledge that mental illness was real and would rave about how it was all a big scam by pharmaceutical companies and psychologists. I never knew what Sarah saw in him, but I also knew that love doesn't always make sense. The heart wants what the heart wants and there is only so much you can do or say when a friend loves someone beyond reason.

When I saw Dave's number on my phone that day in the hardware store, my heart skipped a beat. I knew it could be bad news, but I wasn't expecting what Dave said as soon as I answered: 'Chelsea, Sarah is dead'. The world stopped. I felt like all the air was sucked from my body and I fell to my knees on the floor of the hardware store and burst into tears. Dave and I cried on the phone together for a few minutes until I noticed a crowd starting to gather. I picked myself up off the ground and walked out of the store in a daze.

We had all known there was a chance it could happen, but we had also all hoped that one day she would get the help she needed and would rise up to live the life that we all believed she deserved. It turns out that in her final months she had stopped eating and started drinking even more than she had in the past. Tragically, she had also been introduced to the insidious and destructive drug ice. It was only the week before that I had been talking with her about getting into rehab. I had told her that I would come get her. I offered to pay for it all. We had all been beside ourselves with frustration and anger at her partner's uselessness and her own total lack of self-esteem. While on the phone with her she had been wailing with heartache because her partner had come home and announced that he had met someone else. She felt terrified, abandoned and alone. I tried to tell her that she wasn't alone because she had all of us and we loved her so much, but after years of emotional abuse she couldn't see it. Sarah had been drowning her sorrow with drugs and alcohol. After days of bingeing she had woken up feeling too unwell to drink or take any more drugs. Instead, she went back to bed. My darling Sarah went to sleep and never woke up. Her broken body and shattered heart just gave up.

...

I've come to realise, as much as I hate to admit it to myself, that you can't love anyone enough to fix them or to save them from themselves. All you can do is love them and try to support them as best you can, but the rest is out of your hands.

I started to see that if self-love and self-esteem had never been a part of a child's life, then it could take a lifetime for that child to learn that they are a worthwhile human being, and sometimes that child could grow up and never know how worthy they are of love. Sarah had always been one of my biggest supporters; she believed in everything I was doing. Tragically though, she couldn't believe in herself. There had been so much early damage done to Sarah's sense of herself that, despite all my best efforts and the efforts of the people who truly loved her, she couldn't be saved. Losing Sarah was one of the heaviest blows I have ever experienced, but I feel her spirit with me, right beside me, encouraging me to keep fighting for the changes that can make a difference to someone else's life. When I think of my beautiful friend I try to use my pain to work towards making a difference to the lives of women like Sarah who struggle to believe in themselves. Sarah makes me fight harder every day to let women know they deserve to be loved, no matter what they've been through and no matter what they look like. We are all worthy.

I think that if I hadn't learnt the CBT skills that I did in Thailand I may well have gone back into a dark place after Sarah's death; but using what I had learned about myself at the retreat and all the techniques to keep my mind from free-falling into sadness, I was able to carry on. I miss her like crazy though: my gorgeous red-haired girl with her loud, wild laugh.

CHAPTER 39

After losing Sarah I strengthened my resolve to fight for body-image positivity and to look deeper into how and why women, in particular, feel so disempowered and undervalued in our society. I became more aware of what I, and the people around me, were seeing, reading and internalising and from where the messaging originated. There was one medium that jumped out at me more than the rest and that was social media. The advent of social media has changed the landscape of the fashion and beauty industry, for both good and bad. I do acknowledge that without social media we would never have been able to send out our body love message to so many people or to make as big a mark as quickly as we did with *BELLA*. It's also true that direct access to retailers now means that women can use their voices to communicate publicly. This is fantastic in so many ways, because people can reach out to a public forum and lobby their favourite brands to be more diverse in their advertising practices. We have started seeing more and more comments like, 'Where am I represented? I spend a fortune in your stores!' and we've had customers tag us in posts to retailers saying, 'You should book *BELLA* models!'

On the flip side, however, social media can be a dangerous and underhand medium that ensures anonymity for people with less than good intentions. I once had a mum bring her 15-year-old daughter in to see if she would be suitable for *BELLA*. This young girl had 1.2 million followers on Instagram, so her mother thought she must be the perfect candidate for modelling on the international stage. I looked at this fresh-faced teenager — who was undeniably pretty, but not someone I would scout in the street — and I asked to see her profile online. Most of her images were bikini or lingerie shots. I then showed her mum how to look at the insights, meaning she could see who was looking at the photos of her child. They were nearly all men, from all over the world, and most of them were well over 30. She was horrified.

This is just one example of the ways in which social media skews our industry. There are no guardians at the gate when it comes to social media. In our profession, the agents and managers carefully curate images for portfolios and we vet clients to protect models and talent from those with more underhand intent. Without professional advice or in-depth knowledge of how the modelling industry works, it can be a scary place for the naïve or uninitiated. This young girl thought that her followers were other young women: she did not suspect that most of her 'likes' were coming from dirty old men.

A few years ago we collaborated with Jessica Vander Leahy, founder of Project WomanKIND, to create an online docuseries,'Body Love'. It went viral around the world. #ProjectWomanKIND exposes the honest, real and raw conversations that women have about their bodies, with their girlfriends and in their own heads. It challenges ideals, inspires healthy attitudes and smashes society's narrow definitions of what it means to be truly beautiful. The models, from left, are Sophie Sheppard, Margaret Macpherson, Stefania Ferrario, Jessica Vander Leahy and Olivia Langdon.

Twenty years ago, the diet business was not as profitable as it is now, with much of this relating to the media.

'Media and Body Image', Joel Miller, published online at admedia.com

Where youth were once just exposed to their surrounding peers, they can now readily access the opinions, behaviours, and ideals of thousands of people instantly. There are many online pages, groups, and hashtags that promote disordered eating. Social media can be incredibly dangerous for young people with low self-esteem and distorted body image, since they often find a sense of community and acceptance among online groups that support and encourage their disordered eating.

'How social media affects body image', Brittany Tackett, Project Know, published online at projectknow.com

Social media and the presentation of body image is a brave, but largely unregulated, new world. It can be and is used for good — to spread positivity and self-acceptance — but it is also used as a direct-marketing tool to sell diet products and online weight-loss plans, and often these are presented under the guise of body positivity or healthy living. If you happen to like a page that talks about any of these things, you will be bombarded by suggestions in your feed for more diet plans and more weight-loss products. It won't be long before every time you turn on your social media it tells you, 'YOU ARE NOT ENOUGH'!

Everything from parenting to home styling is marketed on social media and, because it's presented as 'real life', it feeds into a sense of inadequacy if you don't measure up. The images we see on social media appear to be spontaneous and 'real', but they're not. They are meticulously curated and take hours and hours to create. The 'influencers' with extremely high numbers of followers treat the presentation of their images online as a full-time job. They have professional photographers, stylists and content managers curating and designing their image and branding. It's big business and they can often take away huge pay cheques by including products in their shots. I know all this, because I run an influencer board at *BELLA*.

When you look at a picture of a beautiful, young woman eating an açai bowl at her local café, you need to understand it's a form of advertising. NOT REAL LIFE. Some 'influencers' are paid to travel the world and have their picture taken for Instagram. This is a business and it's very lucrative. Even the Instagrammers who don't have a big team behind them are still spending an enormous amount of time planning out content and scheduling the release of images. Models get together and shoot each other to help create content that doesn't cost them a fortune. This is an expected part of the job these days. Clients, the media and the fans want a constant stream of images and ideas in this new world of clickbait and technology-driven sales. We've got to a point where the world won't believe something has happened if it hasn't been posted on social media. It's so exhausting and misleading. It's also dangerous. The more we look at social media images, the more likely we are to compare our lives to what we see online, and that becomes a problem when we think we don't measure up.

The kind of social media we're all exposed to today appeals to our aspirational nature as human beings. We all like to dream; we like to think of ways to better ourselves, improve our lives, strive for more. Looking at beautiful people on social media is a kind of inspiration: it makes us wish we could look like that, live like that. It's okay to dream, but it's a problem when we think the images we are looking at are real. The truth is that nobody's life is like the one they portray on social media.

As an antidote to social media accounts that show beautifully staged images masquerading as real life, I like to follow people who are trying to change the world, not fit into it. I love the pages full of unretouched reality. I love glorious messy humanity, positivity and raw truth. And a wicked sense of humour doesn't hurt either. I feel like our tribe of body image warriors is growing. I'm not alone: there are women and men in the creative and entertainment industries fighting to balance the scales. Together we will find a better way and we will use every win to create another.

EPILOGUE

I look at every shoot and every booking throughout my entire career as special. This is because each one has been part of my journey and has brought me to the place I'm in today. Catalogues to campaign shoots; magazine editorials and covers; television interviews and commercials have all come together to help shift our industry's attitude to body image. I have watched the beauty, fitness and fashion industries embrace a wider size range and I've been so incredibly blessed to be a part of that change. I still love going on set and watching the magic happen, just as I did when I was a child. I'm so proud of the work I do and the people I do it with. It takes a village every day.

Roughly eight months after I was diagnosed with fibro I travelled to Houston, Texas, for the *Sports Illustrated* swimsuit issue launch. I had Mum with me, because she was going to

Studies have demonstrated that more frequent social network use predicts increased body dissatisfaction over time in adolescent girls and boys. Research has also found that a high level of body dissatisfaction is connected to a significant threat to adolescents' well-being.

'The Impact of Social Media Trends on Body Image',
Cindy Cole, *Eating Disorder Hope*, 30 May 2017

come with me to a fibromyalgia treatment centre in Charleston, South Carolina, a few weeks before the launch. I gave Mum an access pass to all the *Sports Illustrated* events, so she could be a part of all the fun. American supermodel Christie Brinkley was featured in the issue with her daughters, so we hung out with her for a while behind the scenes. I loved seeing Mum and Christie chatting, talking about their modelling careers and the similar lives they had led, but on the opposite sides of the world. It was a fantastic trip and I finished up at the event dancing on stage at the closing night party behind the DJ Diplo and alongside the swimsuit models and their teams. As I watched the thousands of people out in the crowd I couldn't stop thinking about what a crazy life of extremes I have experienced and how I wouldn't swap it for anything.

Following this trip, I managed to talk Mum into returning to modelling at 67 years of age. *BELLA* has grown organically into something much more than just an agency working towards representing women whose bodies are larger than a size 10: we had begun to recognise the need to represent women (and men) who pushed the traditional boundaries of age, race, gender and sexuality as well as size. I couldn't be prouder of my models and the diversity we represent. I'm grateful to the people in our industry who understand what we are aiming for and support us.

I've travelled the world doing a job that I love and pushing a cause I believe in. I've met amazing people and done extraordinary things. In just the past year I've been to Perth, Brisbane, Adelaide, Melbourne, Griffith and Byron Bay in Australia and travelled overseas to Charleston, Houston, Dallas, the Bahamas, Thailand, India, London, Dubai and New York. I opened my second agency in South Yarra, Melbourne, I wrote a book and I was invited to give an Australia Day address. I did all of this to carry the message of body image diversity around the world. I'm sometimes criticised for not doing enough, but I've learned not to take it personally and just tell my detractors to get out there and do it themselves. I aim to enjoy my life: I know now I've earned that. I will always continue to try to change and grow the industry for as long as I can.

For me, it has always been a journey about health, both physical and emotional. It's not about society's standards around size: I just want people to be healthy and happy. I receive a fair bit of flak for not having any models over a size 18–20, but this is only because I have yet to meet potential fashion models of that size who are genuinely healthy and well within themselves. I would never sign a size 6 model either, if I could see that she was struggling. I feel it's irresponsible to promote bad eating or an unhealthy attitude to food on both ends of the size spectrum. The long-term effects on a healthy body are much the same at both extremes: blood-sugar issues, joint and bone problems, poor heart function, lethargy and organ failure.

If you are taking care of yourself then that's what's important. No matter what size you are, if you struggle to walk, struggle to breathe, break a sweat going up one flight of stairs, or are tired all the time, then you need to consider some lifestyle changes. I couldn't, in good conscience, sign a model who I knew had these kinds of health issues. I'm trying to promote diversity, but I also want my models to promote good health and happiness.

The most popular social media platforms for young people are Facebook, Instagram, Snapchat and YouTube, and these platforms are predominantly or entirely imaged-based. Because people tend to curate their social media feeds in order to present the best version of themselves on social media, some tend to post only the most attractive images on these sites. Viewing these attractive (and sometimes edited and/or filtered) images of celebrities and friends on social media, and the appearance-related comments these images often receive, has the potential to negatively influence the body image of users.

'Social Media and Body Image', Dr Jasmine Fardouly,
NEDC e-Bulletin, Issue 46

I have friends who are really fit and would still be considered obese by BMI standards. I myself, even in full training for triathlons where I was riding hundreds of kilometres a week, swimming and running every day, was still considered in the obese range according to the BMI standards. I just say, 'Fuck the standards'. If your body is strong and healthy, then it doesn't matter if it doesn't fit into size 8 jeans. Please listen to me when I say I have seen and experienced pretty much everything to do with self-esteem now. Your emotional wellbeing is not connected to your clothing size.

...

Over the past 15 years, *BELLA* models have been a part of game-changing campaigns around the world. My beautiful Stefania Ferrario was the first curvy fashion model in the world to be the ambassador of a major Fashion Week show in my home town of Melbourne. Stefania is also the first size 14 model to shoot with Sportsgirl and as the face of beauty for Myer. My gorgeous Jess King is the face of Jeanswest, which is another amazing move into mainstream retail and beautiful Bree Warren has been the first curve plus-size model to head campaigns for Lorna Jane and Tigerlily and appear on the cover of *Women's Health* magazine. Robyn Lawley was the face of Westfield and a Melbourne Cup Ambassador and has a new range of lingerie and swimwear coming out: a huge step forward for size diversity.

We are seeing a great deal more racial diversity too, with my model Jennifer Atilemile not only booking amazing jobs in Australia, but around the world, heading up campaigns for

Stellar *Magazine 'Legends of the Catwalk' September 2016, with my models Ljubenka, Robyn, Jessica and Sophie, who have become successful leaders of charge and passionate advocates for body image and who represent size diversity and the progression of our industry over the past 25 years.*

Peter Alexander, 17 sundays, Harlow and The Iconic. My girl Jessica Vander Leahy was the first biracial curve plus-size model in Australia and has now featured in campaigns for David Jones and major magazine editorials for *Cosmopolitan*, *Elle* and *Australian Women's Weekly*. La'Tecia Thomas has become an absolute global sensation, launching her own clothing and swimwear line; as has Ljubenka Milunovic, one of Australia's first and most successful curve plus-size models. There are so many wins I could fill another book.

My stunning models are all unique, all different ages, sizes and ethnicities and are shooting all over the world. They are gaining fame, kicking goals and spreading the body-positive message as they go. How is that for a business that the fashion industry thought wouldn't work?

As hard as the filming of *Australian Story* was for me at the time, I will be forever indebted to Lisa McGregor, Vanessa Gorman and their team for opening a door to my own healing and for giving me a chance to show the industry how we can do better. Every single day more and more models of all sizes and ages are coming to us for representation. They are sick of the way they are seen and treated and want to be a part of change for the good.

In 2018 I started what could be my biggest project yet: trying to get a Body Image Warrior program into schools around Australia. It's a huge undertaking, but I'm readier than ever before to take it on. I believe that body confidence should be a fundamental part of our education system and our belief system and I want to prevent another generation of people growing up shrouded in self-hatred; feeling unworthy and

'Fashion brands are rapidly responding to a cultural shift toward body positivity and a growing appreciation of curvy figures, by designing specifically for a larger range of sizes rather than just expanding their size range as an afterthought' — according to a report conducted by management consulting company McKinsey & Co.

'Size does matter: Plus-size fashion gains momentum in 2017', Prachi Singh, *Fashion United*, 22 December 2017

• • •

Children with positive body image might not be completely satisfied with their appearance, but they concentrate on assets rather than flaws. This way of thinking contributes to a positive sense of self-worth. It helps children to detect and fulfil the body's needs, which means they might be more likely to appreciate the value of exercise and make healthy food choices that help the body to perform well.

'Mental Health Matters: Body image', Kids Matter, published online at kidsmatter.edu.au isolated because they can't live up to the extreme ideals of perfection forced into our consciousness every day.

I'm feeling more hopeful than ever before: I can sense a change in the air. There are more and more of us who know the truth, that no-one has it all. Everyone has a struggle that they can't put a filter on and post to social media. It's time to get real with each other and teach our children the same. I speak from experience: I know loss, I've been broken, I'm a woman who's found her way through the ugly truths to uncover beautiful humanity. Contentment is my victory, and I want that for everyone. I hope that my story can help others find peace in themselves.

I have followed my heart and I've worked my arse off: it's been frustrating, terrifying, heartbreaking, joyous and fantastical. I'm so grateful to so many people and I've wanted to knock a few over the head with a frying pan. I wouldn't take a moment back though, not one single second. I'm flawed and passionate, empathetic and no-nonsense. I drink beetroot juice with a cigarette. I'm a human being doing the best I can. I am successful in my business and I'm proud and grateful for that success, mostly because it has allowed me to help so many people. I believe I'm right where I'm supposed to be for now and I'm excited about the next part of my journey and where that might take me. No fear, no anger, no self-loathing. Just me, trying to do my best to leave this joint in a little better shape than when I found it.

Cover shoot for this book! Goofing around with my amazing friends, photographer Michelle Holden and make-up artist Charlie Kielty. It is lovely to work with such talented women who know me so well. Poor Charlie had to move my limbs around for me as I was having such a terrible fibro flare that day and couldn't control my legs. The team kept me laughing for as long as possible, we captured this image and then I went straight home to bed for 14 hours.

ACKNOWLEDGEMENTS

So many people have helped me to get my thoughts together to write this book. My amazing team at BELLA, especially Katherine who took the load from me so I had space to write. Nicole and Sally, who gave me the confidence to pursue it, and friends Russell, Melanie and Claire, who read the earliest drafts and gave me great notes. I could write pages of thank you's so I'll say instead: thank you to everyone who has been a part of my journey, every moment, every conversation, all the love.